We cannot thank God enough for these apparitions

By Patrick McGrath

Transcribed and edited by Helen Loughran
Special thanks to Marian
and Brian

Published by Mourne Books
Banbridge Co Down
©2016

Contents

We cannot thank God enough for these apparitions in Medjugorje	3
My early years and developing in faith and education	4
A new job brings a new relationship with God	8
Preparation for and making my first visit to Medjugorje	14
Organising the first group pilgrimage to Medjugorje from my own area	30
Struggling with my faith in Medjugorje but finding the truth	39
You cannot thank God enough for these apparitions	45
The outbreak of war and travelling to Medjugorje during the war years	59
The all night vigils at Mount Melleray Grotto sows the seed for pilgrimages to Medjugorje	84
The three point break in Bosnia and the cross of sickness	91
Pray until prayer becomes a joy for you	106
Afterword	142
Anyone is capable of going to heaven	145

We cannot thank God enough for these apparitions in Medjugorje

Although many books have been written on this subject, I have become aware that there are people who do not yet know about the events that happened in a rural village in the former Yugoslavia back in 1981. In this book I wish to share with you the story of my own childhood, how my faith developed and how I came to know about the events occurring there over the last twenty or so years.

It was while on a train journey that I met someone who has since become a friend. Through her I became aware that many people don't know much about Medjugorje. I hope to tell the story of these on-going events and how they have changed, and continue to change, the lives of many millions of people. I wish to say that it was Helen who inspired me to write this book and I owe a deep sense of gratitude to her. I hope that those who read this book will be inspired to come to the knowledge and the love of God and to experience His love and His presence in their lives.

My early years and developing in faith and education

I was born on the 13th of December 1960 to my parents Brigid and Pat McGrath, working-class people. My father worked for a local soft-drinks company to help provide for all the needs of the family. There were five of us including my Mother, who worked hard and looked after us in the home. We lived in Chapel Street in the centre of Newry. Shortly after I was born it was discovered that I couldn't see. My eyes had failed to develop due to a condition known as congenital cataracts. It took several operations on my right eye to be able to restore some sight; in my left eye I don't have any sight to this present day. I believe that, soon after my condition was diagnosed, my mother wrote to Padre Pio about my situation. In his reply to her, he said, 'Your son will have enough sight to get around and he will be alright; pray for yourself more, as you are in danger of losing your way'. We lived in the centre of Newry until the end of 1964 when we moved to a new housing estate a mile or so outside of the town, and built on the town land of Derrybeg. This house in Fifth Avenue is where I still live today.

I remember the first time I went into that house, when my father carried me from his big truck up the steps for the first time into our new home. It was shortly afterwards that my youngest brother was born in March '65. Later that year I discovered that I wouldn't be joining my older brother and sister at primary school, I was going to be sent away to a special school in Dublin and in September 1965, my parents took me to this school just outside Blackrock. It was run by the Sisters of Charity and I spent about two years there. It was during this time – which was difficult for me because I was separated from the rest of my family – that the nuns taught us how to pray, along with the normal school subjects which we were to learn gradually.

In September 1968 I was transferred to a boy's school in Drumcondra called St Joseph's, run by the Carmelite Brothers and the Rosminian Fathers. Eventually the Rosminian Fathers took over that school. It was there that my faith was developed. I still remember my early years there, particularly the evenings when we would gather in the church to pray the Rosary. We were given a thorough grounding in catechism and we also learned about the apparitions of Our Lady of Fatima. It was at this school that I first saw the Warner Brothers movie version of the story of Fatima. At that particular time, the teacher was a nun and she reflected on that story with us in the classroom. We were also prepared for confirmation, and taught the usual subjects of reading, writing, and arithmetic, among others.

The discipline of the brothers and priests of St Joseph's was to form me into the person I am today. While there we were told that before we left school we would all have the opportunity to visit Lourdes. The school also had an annual pilgrimage to Knock and we learned about the apparitions that had taken place. I became pals with a number of the other boys there. Like all children, we had recreation and children's games, which we enjoyed a great deal. As the years passed, we learned about the sacraments and the Mass and we were encouraged to go to Mass daily, or at least three times a week. At that time we also had the October devotions, which was a very important part of the school year.

I left St. Joseph's in Drumcondra back in 1977, when I was transferred by the Southern Education Board (part of the Northern Irish system) to an assessment centre in Redhill in the South of England. The centre was called 'Heather Set' and it was run by the Royal National Institute for the Blind. During this particular period of my life I began to want to move away a bit from my faith and explore other things in life. While in England I had an assessment to determine exactly what type of job I would be suited to. They concluded I was most suited to the job of light engineering and inspection. However, I insisted that what I wanted to do was to become a telephonist. This was something I had wanted to do since the time I first operated a switchboard back in St Joseph's in Drumcondra. I remember the first week of doing that job; I knew then that this was the job for me. Little did I know that it would be the job I am still doing up to this present day.

I was in England for one year, during which time I gained the confidence and ability to be able to travel, particularly by air. Looking back, this was all part of the preparation for what God had in store for me later in life. I came back home from England in 1978 and for a couple of years I was unemployed, apart from helping my father out with his soft-drinks delivery. These are some of the best memories I have of my father in life, to which I still cling to this day.

It was in 1980 when a career development officer suggested I apply for a telephonist job which would probably be coming up in the Allied Irish bank in Newry the following year. I agreed that I was interested in this job so a training course was organised for me in August 1980 with a big insurance company in Belfast. I was there for a few months and then called back again at the end of that year to relieve someone else who was on sick-leave. At the close of 1980 and the dawning of 1981, I began a new job in the Allied Irish bank in Newry.

A new job brings a new relationship with God

The bank was situated right opposite the Cathedral. I still remember the first day I arrived at the door and the messenger, who was called Joe, opened the door and showed me into the manager's room. I became acquainted with the staff and began my work as a telephonist on the switchboard, which was situated in the accounts area of the bank. I still remember the staff calling off the account ledgers each day, it sounded to me like a repetitive prayer. Some of the names of the accounts were of the Catholic Churches and schools, reminding me of names that I had been familiar with from school in Dublin.

Later that year an uncle, who I was quite friendly with, got cancer and died at the age of 40. It was the first time that someone close to me had died and this was quite a shock. However as a consequence of his death I discovered that I believed that he had passed on into heaven, that I had faith. I think this inspired me to open my heart to a new relationship with God through Mary.

In June '91, following the death of my uncle, I decided to take a trip to Lourdes - my second visit as I had been previously back in 1973 with my school in Dublin. I remember arriving at Lourdes the first morning, the professional guides from the tour company conducting us to the shrine and giving us a guided tour, explaining to us the various sites of the shrine. I remember visiting the Grotto and the Baths and I took part in the blessing of the sick and the torchlight procession each evening.

The two priests in the group, Fr. Aidan Care from Belfast and Fr. Patrick Searey, a parish priest from Dublin, made me feel very welcome in the group - as they did everyone - and they guided the pilgrimage for four days. I found this to be a wonderful experience. What I got from that trip to Lourdes was an awareness of the sufferings of others and the realisation that my suffering was little or nothing in comparison to others. I discovered, by watching the people lying on stretchers and going to lie down in the baths before the Grotto of Our Lady, that these people had real faith in God and Our Blessed Lady. It turned out that this time I spent in Lourdes coincided with events I will describe later, which began on 24th June. At that particular time in 1981, I was unaware of these events happening in the former Yugoslavia.

This pilgrimage to Lourdes was an important chapter in my life, as I started a new relationship with God. Having been away from the sacrament of Confession for about four years, I now had the opportunity to be reconciled with the sacrament at Lourdes. I attended the Masses each day, which were very beautiful, and the homilies and reflections given by the two priests inspired me deeply. So it came to the end of our pilgrimage and we headed back home to Dublin through the night. Leaving saddened me and I vowed that I would return to Lourdes at some time in the future.

Being back home meant back into my normal routine of life and going to work each day. At work I developed a good relationship with my colleagues, in particular with the two messengers at the bank, Joe and Robert. At weekends I used to go out to dances and various social events with Robert and his wife Mary. The year of '81 rolled by and we moved into '82, when January and February were very cold. I decided early that year that I would take a trip to Rome in order to explore my faith further. It was during this trip that I met Father Michael Duggan of Waterford, a Holy Ghost priest who lived in Dublin. As we made our way on the coach into Rome, he introduced me to Padre Pio. He showed me a mitten that he had and invited me to come to San Giovanni Rotondo the following year. In the hotel he prayed with me for a while, that Padre Pio would intercede for me and maybe restore my sight. It was unbeknownst to me at the time, that my mother had already written to Padre Pio in my early life and had received a letter back from him. In September that year I went back to Lourdes with Fr Michael Duggan and the Holy Ghost fathers and we had a wonderful time there, a prayerful and guided pilgrimage.

I went back to Rome in 1983 with Fr Duggan and a group of people from Waterford and then onward to San Giovanni Rotondo to visit the tomb of Padre Pio for the first time. The four days that we spent there were prayerful and peaceful and inspired me in my faith. Having visited the cell of Padre Pio and the monastery where he lived for over fifty years, I began to understand a bit more about apparitions in general, and also that Padre Pio was visited particularly by Our Lady and his guardian angel, along with other various divine interventions – including visions of the souls in purgatory. I began to read about the life of Padre Pio with the help of my colleague in the bank, Joe Fearon. I brought some books home from San Giovanni and he read them to me day by day. I began to find Padre Pio's life story quite interesting, particularly the spiritual gifts that he manifested, his attacks from the devil and the visitations of Our Lady. I began to listen to taped accounts of his life story. I prayed to him each day for his intercession in my life; that my spiritual life would continue to grow.

It was early in 1984 when I was attending a meeting of the Legion of Mary in my local church that a lady there presented me with a leaflet entitled 'Apparitions of Our Lady behind the Iron Curtain'. The following morning I brought the leaflet with me to work, hoping to get a chance to look at it at some stage during the day. As I was working in my room upstairs in the bank, my colleague Joe came up to visit me and sat with me. He picked up the leaflet and read it himself. When I got an opportunity to have a break from my work, Joe read the leaflet to me. It described the apparitions of Our Lady that began back in 1981 in a rural village in Yugoslavia, called Medjugorje.

The story went on to explain about how Our Lady appeared at the side of a mountain and invited the visionaries to come, introducing herself as Mary Queen of Peace who had come to convert and reconcile. As Joe was reading to me, I had an inspiration - that these apparitions came from God and that one day I was to promote these apparitions. We discussed what we had read and both found it fascinating. I vowed to myself that I would go to Medjugorje one day.

It was in September of that year that I visited Knock for the annual Padre Pio pilgrimage. During the afternoon ceremonies Fr. Jack McArdle, of the Irish office for Padre Pio, spoke about his visit that year to Medjugorje, saying that he'd been privileged to be with the visionaries during the apparition. He explained how he'd witnessed the demonstration of the people from the Vatican who had been sent there to investigate the apparitions and how they were able to test the visionaries during the apparition. He went on to expand on the messages of Our Lady and encouraged the people in the congregation to take seriously and to begin to live the messages. During that talk I made up my mind that I was going to Medjugorje, and whatever happened I was going to get into the apparition room.

It was two years later in 1986 that I first had the opportunity to visit Medjugorje.

Preparation for and making my first visit to Medjugorje

In 1985 I had the opportunity once again of returning to Rome and to San Giovanni on two separate occasions, which I thoroughly enjoyed. I spoke with many people and asked them if they had heard much about the events that took place in Medjugorje. They responded negatively and said that the Church didn't approve of it and that people shouldn't be going there.

In late 1985 I felt that I had a calling to join the priesthood or religious life. I pursued my investigations into this matter and made contact with the local diocesan priest responsible for vocations, who suggested that I might visit the Rosminian novitiate and that he would make contact on my behalf – as they were maybe the best people to train me to follow my vocation. The noviciate's vocations priest set up an appointment for me to visit the noviciate at Easter of 1986, which I did under the guidance of Fr. Mulligan the director of the noviciate in Glencomeragh Co. Tipperary. I spent Holy Thursday, Good Friday, Holy Saturday and Easter Sunday with the Rosminian order and was invited back later that year to spend a fortnight with them during the summer. I went back at the end of July and after a week there, I felt that God was guiding me to go back home, because He had another plan for me there. So with that and without hesitation they brought me back home, which I was happy about. I realised that my vocation was at home, living my Catholic life there.

A few days after arriving back home I got in touch with a friend who told me that she had met some people from my home town of Newry who had visited Medjugorje recently and she invited me to go and see them – they were local publicans – to ask their advice about visiting Medjugorje. I went that afternoon and spoke with Mrs Maddon who showed me some photographs of the visionaries, which meant little to me at the time. Over a pint in her pub, she told me some stories about Medjugorje and encouraged me to go there as soon as possible, as no-one knew how long more Our Lady would be appearing there – after all it had been going on for about four or five years at that time. So at work the following day I contacted another friend, a lady called Carmel Smith, and suggested to her that she might like to come with me to Medjugorje. Initially Carmel didn't think she would come along; she didn't have the money and really wasn't interested. However, about thirty minutes later she called me back and said, 'Patrick, I think I would be interested in going, could you arrange the trip for us? My Aunt Molly would like to come with me as well'.

I said, 'Certainly Carmel, leave it with me and I'll see what I can do'.

So I contacted the travel agent in Dublin – Concorde Travel – who was arranging trips to Yugoslavia, running flights every Saturday night to Medjugorje. I spoke with a colleague at work about the trip; he consulted with the Dublin branch of the bank we worked for who endorsed the travel company. With that Carmel and I started to arrange a trip beginning on the 20th September 1986.

The evening came when we were to depart on our pilgrimage; we left Newry by car and drove up to Dublin airport through the rainy night. We arrived at the airport in time to check in for our flight which was to depart at 1AM. We boarded our flight, along with a group from Donegal and a number of people from Dublin. Our plane was full and ready to take off. We headed into the night sky flying across Europe. Dawn broke and we could see the Adriatic Sea as the plane descended towards Split. At sunrise we landed at Split, at that time behind the Iron Curtain. To us this was a new country we'd never been to before. We were tired with no sleep during that night. We were hustled through passport control and the baggage-reclaim area, out into the main airport building where we boarded buses.

Our guide advised us we'd stay in little guest houses and suggested we get some rest; she would meet us later that afternoon for an introductory meeting. As we drove up through the countryside and the mountains, some of us began to nod off as we had been awake all night. On our arrival at Medjugorje, my first impression was of partially finished buildings – there wasn't much to the place. The bus made its way into the village, along the narrow streets and over the one-vehicle wide bridge. We turned up into a little dirt-track that led up to the church, which was all that was there at the time.

After a few exchanges, we were driven to a number of houses where we dropped people off. Eventually it was our turn to get off the bus. Having been sitting on the bus for about four and a half hours we were exhausted and in need of something to drink, and some of us were in need of a smoke as well. So we were hastened into our houses. There were around twelve people in our house, in those days it was three to a room and four or five to one bathroom. We were happy enough to have a cup of tea and then go to bed for a few hours to have some rest. Later that afternoon we assembled outside the front entrance of the church under the trees, where there were some benches. The guide from Concorde Travel, who worked in Medjugorje, introduced us to another lady from Dundalk who was based there to help out the

Franciscans with the English speaking pilgrims. She introduced us to the shrine and told us some bits and pieces about the place itself and what to expect during the coming week. After that we gathered outside the room of the parish office where we were told the apparition of Our Lady would take place. So we began to pray the Rosary there and we noticed the visionaries going inside for the evening apparition.

The first evening we simply attended Mass. During the Mass there was a power cut and we could just about hear the Mass from outside. Afterwards we went back down to the accommodation, where we had our evening meal served to us. All of us being so tired, we turned in for the night.

The next morning we had breakfast, left our various houses and headed through the fields once again to the church of St. James, where we had English Mass at 10 o'clock. After Mass we gathered outside the church where the tour guide wished to have an information meeting with us, to give us an idea of the programme for the remainder of the day and the rest of the week. After the meeting it was decided among the group that we have a short break for refreshments, after which we headed to the vineyards at the foot of the mountain where the first apparitions had begun. We began to pray the Rosary as we walked through the fields, watching the local farmers pick grapes for the harvest to make wine.

Approaching the base of the small mountain, we paused for an intermission and then climbed the rocky terrain to the site of the apparition. On our way up we asked one another why it was that the visionaries came up this hill to see Our Lady. When we arrived at the site of the apparition the story of the early days was explained to us by the group of priests there and we learned that on the 24th of June 1981, while going for a walk, six young people saw Our Lady. They were: Vicka, Maria, Marie-Anna, Evan, Jakov and Ivanka. They saw a vision of a lady standing at the spot we had arrived at. The lady waved at them and invited them to come closer. She uncovered an infant in her hands and then covered it up again. The visionaries were so frightened that they ran away. The following day, the same six went to the same area for a walk, as they felt that something was drawing them there. Once again they saw the vision of Our Lady; she was wearing a grey dress and a white robe and she looked quite young. She stood on a cloud. She waved at them inviting them to come closer, and within minutes they were at the spot where we had ourselves arrived. After that short story we began to pray the Rosary and walked back down to the base of the hill.

All of this took some considerable time, so at that stage we decided we would have some refreshment and go back to our houses for the afternoon, as the heat of the day had left us feeling drained. In the evening we returned once again to the church for the Rosary. In those days the apparition took place in the parish house of the priest Father Slavko Barbaric, so we gathered at the foot of the steps to the presbytery, hoping that there might be an opportunity to get in and to be with the visionaries. However, when the priest in charge of the room came to the bottom of the steps, he closed the gate and said that only sick people and priests would be admitted that evening, as there were too many of us clamouring to get in.

They began the Rosary at about six o'clock and we participated outside, led by one of the groups. About forty minutes later, the light outside the presbytery door came on, which signified to us that the apparition was taking place. A silence came over the area and we knelt in silent prayer. After the apparition the doors were opened, the visionaries came down and were hustled away quickly to the church. We moved up the pathway to the church, where we sat outside and tried to participate in the Croatian Mass – a language which was completely new to us. After Mass we knelt for the Common Prayer, which is now said every evening; the Creed, seven times the Our Father, Hail Mary, Glory Be and thanksgiving; the healing prayers and the glorious mysteries. Afterwards we went back to our various houses where we had our evening meal and sat for quite a while, sharing and talking, having a bit of general craic and sampling the wine which the local people had put up for us at our meal. Once again it was time to retire.

The following morning we had breakfast, and then out once again through the fields back to the church of St James for the English Mass. After Mass we had another information meeting with the tour representative who told us that we might have an opportunity to meet one of the visionaries later that day. However that wasn't possible, instead we decided that during that day we would take a walk over to the Blue Cross area, located at the base of the Apparition Hill. On the way there by chance we met one of the visionaries, Vicka, who happened to be living in that area at the time and was doing some chores around her garden. She paused for a while, we had our photographs taken with her and she prayed with us. Then we went on up to the Blue Cross, which denotes the place where Our Lady first appeared.

Later we went back into the centre of the village, where we stopped for some lunch, before returning to our houses to take a rest in the afternoon heat. On our way back a couple of local elderly men stopped in their tractors and offered us some grapes, as it was harvest time and they had plenty. Then, on arriving back at the house, we were offered some wine, water or tea and rest. In the evening we returned to the foot of the presbytery steps, hoping for a chance to get into the apparition.

Once again the priest came to the bottom of the steps, closed the gate and said that only the sick and priests would be admitted. We began to pray the Rosary in preparation for the apparition. At 6:40 the light came on again, signifying the apparition was about to take place, so we knelt in silent prayer. After this the visionaries came out and were hustled away to the church for the Croatian Mass once again. However on this second evening, rather than sitting outside at the side of the church, we went around to the back, which was just simply a field. When we got there, we saw what looked to be the silhouette of a lady whose palms were outstretched over the church in the sky. This we believed to be Our Lady. It was as if Our Lady had taken the form of the colour of the sun. It was white, her hands were outstretched and it was like the sun was setting below her. This sight lasted for quite a while and after a few moments we decided that we would pray the Rosary. A number of us saw this sight that evening and we were certainly privileged to be able to witness it.

Towards the end of the Rosary, the vision disappeared back into the sky and everything returned to normal. In those days there were many reports of various manifestations. Some people said that they saw the miracle of the sun which was first shown in Fatima in 1917; where the sun danced and pulsated through the sky, changing to different colours, from orange to blue to green. Others said they saw the big cross at the top of Cross Mountain disappearing and fire taking its place. Some people said they saw the cross illuminated when there weren't any people up there to make that happen. It's not certain whether some of these sightings are true or false; I don't wish to make any judgement on that.

After these events we went back to our houses. There was nothing to do after the evening prayer programme so we had our meal and sat around the table, sampling the wine, having some craic and making the best of the evening. The following morning we headed out through the fields to English Mass. At the information meeting it was decided that we would do the Stations of the Cross while climbing the Cross Mountain. At about two o'clock in the afternoon we left the centre of the village, walked towards the base of the Cross Mountain and began to climb. This I found quite difficult; however I managed to accomplish the climb. We stopped at each of the fourteen Stations of the Cross and reflected. Having climbed to the top we felt a great sense of achievement, as Cross Mountain is roughly about 900 feet above sea level. We stayed there for a short while before making our descent down the rocky mountain back to the base. When we returned to the village of Medjugorje, I decided that it would be a good idea to help to bring a group here from my own area at home.

We went once again to the apparition at the presbytery, where we all gathered in hope and anticipation that we might get in this evening. However once again the priest came to the gate and admitted only a few sick people and priests, he closed the gate then and said, 'No more', since there were already enough people in the small room. We prayed the Rosary there and the light went on at 6:40 signifying the pause for the apparition. This period of pausing lasted for five to seven minutes, after which time the light went off, the visionaries came out to their place in the church. This time I went inside the church because I wanted to experience the beautiful music and the atmosphere of the Mass. The church was so packed that there were no seats, I had to stand throughout the Mass. When I got the opportunity, for instance during the homily of the Mass, I sat on the floor like so many others. The atmosphere inside the church was beautiful and the singing and chants of the Croatian Mass were always in my mind throughout the days after I left Medjugorje.

After the thanksgiving prayers, we headed back towards our little pansion / boarding houses where we had our evening meal and sat around the table sharing what we had experienced throughout that day. The following morning, being Thursday, the week was drawing to a close and once again we headed out after breakfast through the fields to Mass. I remember it was quite a wet morning and we had our English Mass and then the information session. Because of the weather it wasn't possible to carry on with what we had planned, so we just sat around, had some burgers and refreshments, while sharing our experience of the pilgrimage so far. In the afternoon it stopped raining, so we went for a walk through the fields to the base of the Apparition Hill (the Blue Cross), where we shared some prayers. We came back again that evening for the Rosary. This was followed by same procedure at the base of the presbytery, we gathered in hope and anticipation that we'd get in. Again we prayed in silence and then went back to the church for the evening Mass.

Friday came, the last day of our pilgrimage before we were due to depart. Friday morning I remember was quite wet and we walked through the muddy fields for the English Mass. During the information session afterwards we were told of the details of our departure the following day and that one of the visionaries, Vicka, would be having a formal meeting with us that afternoon. After lunch the weather cleared up again and we went across to the foot of the Apparition Hill where Vicka lives. Vicka came out and shared with us the divine messages that Our Lady had spoken to her, as well as her experiences of the apparitions. Because I had a disability and a couple of others in the group were sick, the priest in the group invited us to come forward and allowed Vicka to pray with us. This I thought was a great privilege. After the meeting we headed back through the fields to the church area in the centre of the village.

When I arrived back at the base of the presbytery my friend Carmel, who had travelled with me but had not come for the meeting with Vicka, asked me where I was going. I said I needed to go and use the bathroom, but she replied, 'You're not going there - you're going into the apparition room!' I said, 'How do you know?' She had asked the priest in charge of the room to let me in. 'I told him about your situation, about you being blind and that sort of thing and the priest said if you bring him he will get in'. So I had to stand for about half an hour before the priest came and opened the gate. I was dressed in a black jumper and a grey jacket.

While we were waiting there, Carmel said that maybe the guy who would open the door might think that I was a priest. I said that I couldn't do that; going in there under false pretences. So anyway, when the priest in charge of the apparition room came to the bottom of the steps and opened the gate, he said, 'Priests and sick people only'. There was an American priest, who I'd become acquainted with, standing behind me and I said to him, 'Father you go before me because you're a priest' and he replied abruptly to me, 'You go because if you don't move I'll not get in!' So I moved up the steps and he moved behind me and into the apparition room.

An Irish priest who had been travelling with us – he'd got to know me well - greeted me and instructed me to have a seat in the centre and advised, 'Just don't say anything'. So the doors were closed and I was inside in the room along with a number of other priests. We began to pray the Rosary and shortly afterwards the visionaries Maria and Jakov came in, knelt and began to pray with us. At about 6:40 or thereabouts the two visionaries got up simultaneously and went to the centre of the room where they fell on their knees and went into the apparition. It's hard to describe exactly what took place there, as all I could see was their heads going back and their hands joined in deep prayer. They were obviously seeing something and I've no doubt it was Our Lady. After a few moments they bowed their heads and came out of the ecstasy. They then prayed the Magnificat, after which Father Slavko said to us that now it was time to go to the church. So we left the room, went down the steps and then headed down to the church for Mass.

After Mass a number of people who had seen me going into the room asked me what I had experienced and I was able to give an account of the experience of being in the apparition room. This was my two-year-old ambition, to get to Medjugorje and to be present with the visionaries during an apparition. So I was quite excited and delighted to have achieved this; it was very special.

We went back to our boarding houses once again, had our evening meal and retired for the night. The following morning we prepared ourselves for our journey back home that evening; however we had most of the day in Medjugorje. It's worth mentioning that on the last day we had a meeting with one of the two Inner Locutionists, this is someone who is receiving a message inwardly from, in this case Our Lady, or the Holy Spirit. This is something that I had great difficulty in understanding, but the messages that they've been given – like Basil who was the Inner Locutionist who met us that day – were quite similar to the messages that were being given to the visionaries at the apparitions. I was to have this experience myself. In a later chapter in this book I shall write about my own experience of having an inner locution and receiving a lot of inspirations. That was the end of my first pilgrimage to Medjugorje. It had a long lasting effect. During the days after I arrived back home, I felt that I had been in such a holy place and hoped and longed to return there in the not too distant future.

Organising the first group pilgrimage to Medjugorje from my own area

About a month after we had returned home from our first trip to Medjugorje, I approached my friend Carmel, who had already been there with me, and suggested that she might help me to take a group out there the following year. Reluctantly, Carmel agreed to give me assistance with this, so we sought a travel agent in Dublin who was offering special flights directly from Dublin to Mostar. We met with the agents themselves in November of that year and they proposed that we take a group of fifty. They explained to us that they had acquired an airliner costing four million, a Boeing 727, which would enable them to fly the pilgrims into Mostar – about a half hour from Medjugorje. We agreed a price with them and early the following year we began to advertise our trip in the local paper. Within a couple of days of advertising we had a good response and one week after our first advert we already had approximately fifty people! We suggested to the tour operator that we might need more seats and eventually we gathered about ninety-four persons from around the area and from different parts of the country as well. The pilgrimage was organised for the fifteenth of July 1987 – the following year.

On that day we took off around lunchtime. On our approach to the airport at Mostar, the pilot told us that the temperature was about 37 degrees Celsius on the ground. So it was a new experience again for me and many of the others on board as we'd never been in such a hot climate. When the plane landed, we disembarked and found ourselves walking into a rush of heat as we assembled on the tarmac. Mostar airport was a military airport and some of the equipment was still lying around there. The airport authorities were anxious to get us through the various procedures, passport and customs control, as quickly as possible; out onto the bus and away from the airport.

About half an hour later, roughly about half past six in the evening, we arrived at Medjugorje once again, back into the old village that we had left about eight months previously. We found a few changes there on arriving; however first we were allocated to our various houses. Because there were so many in the group we had a number of houses and it was hard to keep in touch with everyone. The information meeting each morning after Mass was about the only time we could see the whole group, as we were scattered about in different parts of the village.

Acclimatising to the heat was difficult for all of us. With temperatures of about forty degrees Celsius, we had to drink plenty of fluids and it took us a day or so to get used to that. On the first morning, as on previous pilgrimages, we congregated in the church for English Mass at ten o'clock. This was an uncomfortable experience because it was so hot and there were so many people in the small church, which had no air conditioning in those days. We had to use towels continually to wipe the perspiration from our faces.

That particular week, I was given the responsibility of leading the singing of the congregation at the English Mass, which was a great privilege for me. In the group we had a number of priests and one of them was from my home area, in fact he had worked with me in the church in my own parish in Newry. So as we moved through the week of warm weather, the procedure was the same as before. Once again we waited in hope and anticipation every evening that we would get into the apparition room. It was too warm to climb the mountains during the day, though some of us undertook the ordeal at night. One of the highlights of that week was that around midnight on the third night, a number of us decided to climb Cross Mountain. We did so, stopping at each station of the cross and reflecting. There were two priests from Limerick with us and when we reached the summit of Cross Mountain; as someone had brought a bottle of wine and some of us had some bread, they decided that they would use the bread and wine to offer holy

Mass. This was a nice experience and it lasted for about forty-five minutes.

A day or so later, I was to learn that what we'd done on Cross Mountain was against the law in that country, because it was still under the communist regime. It was also against Church law which went in accordance with state law - that Masses could not be offered up privately and apart from the public Masses in the church. We found this unusual, as in Ireland we have a more liberal religious law.

However, the week progressed and with the weather being warm, on the Saturday a number of us decided to take a trip down to the coast, down to a place called Makarska. There the weather was like a breath of fresh air and we had the chance to have a dip in the Adriatic Sea. When we arrived back that evening, I learned that one of the pilgrims in the group, who had been ill, had apparently died suddenly that morning. This brought a bit of sadness to the group. We went and sympathised with her sister, who had accompanied her. Tragically, that evening we also learned that a young teenager from Drogheda, who had gone for a swim in the waterfall a few days previously, had sadly drowned. This put the agency and the guides, who had to deal with the two deaths within the space of a few days, under enormous pressure.

The following morning we offered Mass for the two pilgrims who had died, as the priest from our local parish was the main concelebrant of the Mass. The situation was that the pilgrimage went on as normal and the sister of the lady who'd died told us that despite her loss she felt very happy within herself – she knew that her sister had passed into heaven.

One of the good things that came out of that week was the fact that I was able to help bring so many people to Medjugorje who had never been there before. It's very satisfying to know that you have helped people to come to know God in a better way, to experience the peace and to begin to live the message of Medjugorje. When we went back home after the July pilgrimage I felt that it would be nice to organise a second group later that year. We did so in the middle of October - both myself and Carmel. It was a smaller group and we had a local priest with us as well. It was an opportunity for me to begin to take seriously the messages of Our Lady and to be able to participate in each evening programme, even though it involved long periods of standing in the church during the Rosary and the evening Mass, which still seemed strange in a different language.

Even though I'd been there twice before, Medjugorje was still a relatively new experience for me. We had a great second week there in October. Again we had a few people who had never been there before and others who had been in July and come back again because they felt they wanted another chance to enjoy the atmosphere there. I can only describe Medjugorje as basically a place of prayer and of holiness, and in those days a place of simplicity. The people there at that time were poor, had little or nothing and their main source of income was probably selling tobacco and harvesting the grapes. The pilgrims were beginning to become a source of income for them as well, although being under the former Yugoslavian regime, the government cashed in a bit, they took a third of the income that the pilgrims were giving to the local people, who had originally opened their homes for nothing in the earlier years.

On that second trip in October '87, there had been a change in the situation regarding the apparition. On the 25th July 1987 the bishop of Mostar came in to give Confirmation to the local parish. In Medjugorje there has always been an aggressor of one kind or another. In the early days it was the communist authorities who tried to prevent people from going there, to prevent public worship on the Apparition Hill and the Cross Mountain and in some cases confining and even arresting people for having prayer services on the Apparition Hill etc. Also, in the early years, the bishop of Mostar had believed in Medjugorje and the apparitions at first, but the twelve diocesan clergy approached him one day and persuaded him not to believe that Our Lady would appear in a Franciscan parish, awakening an old dispute that had lasted over a hundred years.

For five hundred years of Turkish occupation, the Franciscans had been the only priests who had remained in that region in order to look after the faithful. A lot of them were arrested and subsequently killed / burned, but those who were saved were protected by the people themselves. They used to call the brown-robed friars their uncles. However at the turn of the century when the diocesan priests decided to return after the Turkish occupation had desisted, a number of people in the now Franciscan-run parishes didn't accept them, as the Franciscans had been their guardians for over five hundred years. This dispute seemed to resurrect itself when the apparitions of Medjugorje began and when the twelve diocesan priests approached the then bishop of Mostar to persuade him not to believe in the them.

This came to the fore on the 25th of July 1987, when the bishop issued a statement during the Confirmation service, that the apparitions in Medjugorje and the happenings there were part of the work of the devil. This caused a tremendous backlash until the Vatican intervened and told the Franciscans they were to continue with what was going on in Medjugorje. The bishop tried to ban international language Masses in the village, much to the dislike of many people and the Vatican authorities.

The situation persisted for many years. One of these twelve priests, in fact the ring-leader, was Father Ratko Peric who later became the bishop of Mostar. As bishop he remained in opposition against the happenings at Medjugorje and continued to be very strict with the Franciscans. In spite of all that however, the prayerful atmosphere in Medjugorje still goes on. The Franciscans remain the guardians of the parish and they continue to look after both the faithful people of Medjugorje and pilgrims who go there. The important thing to remember is that even though the Church has not officially approved of the apparitions of Medjugorje, neither has it disapproved, but it does permit the faithful to travel there as private individuals on private pilgrimage. It also permits the international and various language Masses and the reception of the sacraments, particularly the sacrament of reconciliation and Confession, which we'll talk a little bit about later on.

After the statement of July 25th, the bishop of Mostar ordered that the apparitions no longer take place on Church property. Despite this the friars decided, in the best interests of everyone, that they would allow the visionaries to come into the church, as no-one has any right to stop anyone coming into the church to pray. They allowed the visionaries to have the apparitions in the choir loft, where the choir sings at the moment, and the apparitions took place there until about four or five years ago (current 2010).

So, that was the change that we found, instead of having to gather at the bottom of the steps of the presbytery, as we had before, we were all able to go into the church and pray. The one thing that we found distracting was that during the pause for the apparition, many people turned around to look and some took photographs. However, on a number of occasions I was present on the balcony, and we'll speak about that a bit later on in the chapters referring to the war.

Struggling with my faith in Medjugorje but finding the truth

After returning home from Medjugorje in October '87, myself and Carmel organised a pilgrimage for the following year. However as early 1988 approached, we discovered that the numbers of people we anticipated would travel was to be a lot less this year than last year. I began to question my belief in the apparitions in Medjugorje and I suppose I was listening to too many of my friends who didn't believe them. I wanted to go there but felt I couldn't. I ended up visiting Lourdes on two occasions in 1988 but realised that this wasn't what I was looking for. Eventually, having been absent from Medjugorje for twelve months, I returned there in October 1988. That was a year of struggle in faith for me; claims and counter-claims of apparitions elsewhere being part of the reason. However when I returned to Medjugorje, my faith in the apparitions was rekindled.

It was the first time that I had the opportunity to visit Father Jozo Zovko, who was parish priest in Medjugorje when the apparitions first began in 1981. We learned about the early days during that visit, Father Jozo told us various stories in connection with the apparitions and his experience as parish priest in Medjugorje at the beginning. He spoke particularly of the eighth day, he was in the church praying for guidance when he heard a voice speak to him. The voice, he said, was an acoustic voice that told him to go and protect the children, which is what he did. He opened the church door and found the children being chased by the police, so he took them in and hid them in a room. He also told other stories, such as being in the church in the early days and asking people to make their sign of peace with each other. It happened that there was a man in the church who hadn't spoken to another gentleman at the far end of the church for about twenty or thirty years. When Father Jozo, during the Mass, asked the people to pray for peace and asked them to extend their hands to each other, this man embraced the other man and asked for forgiveness for not speaking for so long.

Father Jozo also spoke about conversions and inexplicable healings, which he said were always present when there were authentic apparitions from God, as in Lourdes and Fatima. He told a story of how he had once encountered a gentleman on a stretcher in the church area of Medjugorje and he told the man, 'Jesus heals you, get up' and immediately the man got up off his stretcher. This was something we discovered about Father Jozo; he had a tremendous power of healing. After the talk, he blessed the priests first of all and empowered them to deliver their blessing to the people in the congregation. This is the first time that I witnessed what's known as 'The Resting in the Spirit', when Father Jozo and the priests prayed over the people and a number of the people fell to the ground; this was the power of the Holy Spirit. It was something new for me, and a bit frightening, but as time went on, I began to understand that this was only given to people who need it, and that the others who didn't receive it, didn't need it at that particular time.

Having listened to Father Jozo, my faith in the apparitions began to be restored. I left Medjugorje renewed in my belief in the apparitions and returned home to live the message. Also, each day I read one of Our Lady's messages. Our Lady gave the messages each Thursday from 1984 until 1987, after which on the 25th of every month - and still does so. I found reading the message a source of strength and above all it was encouraging me to integrate the message into my life. This I did as I resumed my work back at home each day as 1988 drew to a close.

In 1989 I visited Medjugorje on three occasions; in the spring, summer and late autumn. I helped to accompany a number of other pilgrims to Medjugorje during that year. I noticed a number of changes in the place, for example there were a lot more buildings going up and the accommodation was improving for the pilgrims, although many of us still had to stay about 20 minutes to a half an hour's walk from the church. This we didn't mind since we were happy to be in such a holy place.

August '89 was the time of the first youth prayer festival that was held in Medjugorje and was led by the late Father Slavko Barbaric. There were a few hundred young people there and I remember that occasion well. It coincided with the feast of the Assumption of Our Blessed Lady on 15th of August. It was the first time I was there for that feast. The weather was hot but there was a lovely prayerful atmosphere during the festival. The youth festival basically consists of talks given by the visionaries and the priests. Usually beginning at nine o'clock in the morning with a full programme until about noon, they then resume at four o'clock with talks given by some of the priests and by some of those who bear witness to having been healed or converted in Medjugorje. Then it moves on into the evening prayer programme, with the Rosary at six o'clock followed by the Mass at seven. The Adoration of the Blessed Sacrament took place every night and lasted for about an hour, there was a lovely atmosphere during it.

Today, twenty years later, the youth festival is still going and the crowds have grown now to about four thousand young people. I was there recently for it and there was a tremendous atmosphere of faith. It's wonderful to see so many young people gathered together in prayer, but it's also a time of joy – not all prayer – there's time for people to meet each other, socialise and enjoy each other's company.

In October '89 I brought a small group of people from my own area, accompanied by one of our local priests. During the pilgrimage the weather became inclement; there was a lot of heavy rain. On one occasion I remember we attended a talk in the newly constructed dome, given by Ivan the visionary. Ivan would usually speak about the main messages that Our Lady has called us to live by, calling us to pray, to fast, to go to Mass and to attend confession once a month, he would also speak to the people about his experiences of Our Lady's apparitions. He would then usually allow the people to ask any questions they had. Sometimes people would ask questions such as, 'Does Our Lady ever say anything about how we should receive Holy Communion, whether it be in the hand or on the tongue?' Ivan's answer basically was, 'The Church allows on the hand or on the tongue, the choice is there'. Another question was, 'Does Our Lady say anything about America or about Ireland?' to which he'd reply, 'No, Our Lady does not say anything about any particular country, Our Lady's messages are for the whole world' These questions sometimes caused a bit of disquiet amongst the people. However with Ivan's calmness it didn't take away from their enthusiasm.

Also in 1989 I was introduced for the first time to the Devotion of the Divine Mercy, which was a revelation by Jesus himself to a polish nun in Krakow called Faustina, now canonised as Saint Faustina. It was on a Thursday afternoon when Father Phillip, the American priest who took charge of the English liturgy in Medjugorje, conducted a holy hour and he chanted this beautiful chaplet of Divine Mercy – a chant that I was to use a few years later in one of my own local churches, when we started the first Divine Mercy devotion in St Catherine's in Newry, sometime around 1993.

The pilgrimage of October '89 came to an end and we headed back home, and as the year itself drew to a close I had discovered that Medjugorje was not simply about bringing other people there, it was also about how I should live the message itself in my own life. So I began to concentrate more on that, simply by reading and by living the programme, the three parts of the Rosary and attending holy Mass as often as possible, usually once a day.

You cannot thank God enough for these apparitions

Medjugorje Message, November 25, 1990

'Dear children! Today I invite you to do works of mercy with love and out of love for me and for your and my brothers and sisters. Dear children, all that you do for others, do it with great joy and humility towards God. I am with you and day after day I offer your sacrifices and prayers to God for the salvation of the world. Thank you for having responded to my call.'

In March 1990 I remember being asked by one of the local priests here in Newry if I would accompany and help him to sing at a funeral Mass which he was to conduct that particular day. This I did and after attending the funeral I found myself asking a lot of questions about my faith and about the hereafter. For a period of time I suppose I began to have doubts about my faith. Maybe this was to prepare me for what was to come a little later that spring. I visited Medjugorje in the first week of May 1990 and for the first couple of days it was difficult for me to tune in to the spirit of prayer. The week drew to a close and in fact I felt it was no longer necessary for me to come to Medjugorje. I withdrew from a lot of the activity there, until the evening before I was due to return home. As I was praying the Rosary outside the church during the evening programme, I heard this inner voice say to me, 'I want you to come here more often'. Inwardly I answered the voice by saying, 'But Blessed Mother I come here often enough'. However the voice, who I believed to be the Blessed Mother, said back to me, 'Still I want you to come here more often'. The following day, as I was getting ready to leave Medjugorje that evening, I felt happy and very much at peace, for the first time since I arrived. In fact, I felt a tremendous sense of peace about myself.

I left Medjugorje to fly home late into the night, arriving back into Dublin about one or two o'clock in the morning. That day I got up rather late and I remember turning on the television and watching the remains of the late Cardinal O'Fee being brought home from Lourdes, where he had died that week. It wasn't until a week or so later that things started to happen and change the direction of my life completely regarding Medjugorje.

During that first week at home I found it difficult to settle in again and I had a great desire to go back to Medjugorje. At Mass on the Sunday a week after being at home, I was assisting with the singing in my local church and the nun who conducted the group had given me instructions as to what hymns they were to do. She did not tell me, or I believed that she did not intend, that we should sing the Our Father.

However, when we came to the end of the Eucharistic prayer, during the singing of the Amen, an inner voice said to me, 'Why don't you sing the Our Father?' At that moment I wasn't in a position to do anything about it, but when I turned towards the group, I saw the nun instructing them to play the Our Father. This amazed me; in fact it actually shocked me as obviously she'd had a similar inspiration. However, I managed to sing the Our Father, making one or two mistakes that I'm sure went unnoticed. It was during Holy Communion that an inner voice told me again, 'Your prayer has been answered'. Well I didn't know what my prayer was until the following morning.

That night I had a dream and in the dream I was in the apparition room along with the visionaries during the apparition. It was a tremendous experience and felt very real. I woke from the dream and as I lay there in bed in the bright Spring morning, suddenly I heard a voice say to me, 'Patrick, you cannot thank God enough for these apparitions'. This repeated it must have been about a dozen times! And every time I heard this voice my heart filled with joy, my whole being filled with joy. I got up and got ready for work. Before I left I looked at the mail that had arrived and there was a letter from the travel agency. I opened it and written in letters big enough for me to read, it said, 'Special offers for Medjugorje'. They gave prices for one and two week stays and they were good prices. I put the letter in my pocket and went on to work.

At work that day it wasn't so busy; I took the letter from my pocket and proceeded to read it, having in mind to ring someone else to inform them of the cheaply priced pilgrimages to Medjugorje. As I was reading the letter, I heard the inner voice again saying to me, 'It would be better for you to go now rather than later'. This took me by surprise, so I put the letter back into my pocket and thought that the best thing to do about this voice that I was hearing was to pray for guidance. Since work wasn't busy, I decided to take my little Rosary and pray. Quietly I did so. During the Rosary, the voice said, 'It's better for you to go now rather than later. It won't be so busy now and you can do what you like with your holidays'. When I had finished praying, I turned to a calendar of Padre Pio on the wall beside me to pick out what dates I wanted to go. As I did so, it was as if Padre Pio said to me, 'Go now, rather than later'. So I made up my mind to go from the 9th to 23rd of June.

The next obstacle was to seek permission to get time off work, as I'd only just come back from Medjugorje. So at lunchtime I approached the staff officer and suggested that I would like to take an early summer holiday. To her this seemed to be no problem whatsoever. She asked me for the dates and agreed to arrange cover for me during those two weeks.

I didn't know what I had been called for, so as I was working across the road from the cathedral, I decided to go over and pay a visit to the Blessed Sacrament and thank God for whatever it was that he had chosen me for. I felt very happy about this and couldn't wait to get to Medjugorje. I remember that evening going to Mass in my local church and, as soon as I approached the inside of the church, a great joy came over me. I had accepted the will of God. During the month of June I prepared to go to Medjugorje. I left Newry and headed for Dublin airport once again, this time for a fortnight. I'd never been in Medjugorje for more than a week, so this was a new experience for me as well.

When I arrived in Dubrovnik that night, the guide who had accompanied me to the airport a month previously, met me off the plane and asked what was I doing back there so soon. I just said, 'I'm here', and the guide said to me, 'Well you've come at the right time, it will not be very busy now, it's just before the anniversary so you've picked a good time to come'. And it was a good time.

I usually went into the church at about five or ten minutes to six each evening, in preparation for the Rosary. Normally at that time, just before the Rosary, you would never have been able to get a seat but it was as if there was a seat being held for me every evening. On several occasions during the evening Rosary, I heard the voice again, 'I have chosen you for this, your prayers are necessary to me'. This is how I knew that it was Our Lady speaking to me. Quite often I get inspirations, which I believe are coming from Our Lady, maybe the source is my Guardian Angel, I'm not sure but they always inspire me to do good and it's a good situation to be in.

That particular week it was the feast of Corpus Christi. We in Ireland are used to having processions and freedom of religious expression, but back in those days in the former Yugoslavia, although the federation was beginning to break up, public worship or processions were not permitted on the public street. On the eve of Corpus Christi, I was halfway down the aisle of the church for the 7pm Mass when I saw a priest coming out from the altar. There were several priests on the altar at that time. I saw the main concelebrant coming out and before he could actually speak, I was told in an inspiration that this was Father Jozo and as soon as he spoke I recognised his voice. I heard Father Jozo preach like I've never heard any priest preaching before or since. Even though I didn't understand a lot of what he was saying he got my attention as well as everybody else's. Everyone's eyes in the church were fixed on him, his preaching was profound and he spoke in a loud voice in order to get the attention of the people there.

It happened that the following morning on the feast of Corpus Christi itself, we were to leave to go to Father Jozo's parish of Tihilina for his talk and healing service. This we did, leaving at about seven o'clock and getting there just before eight. We were there for the beginning of his Mass and again it was a privilege, because during the previous Mass I had been told in an inspiration that Father Jozo wasn't just an ordinary priest, he was very special. After the Mass, he gave us a talk on the feast of Corpus Christi and on the real presence of Jesus in the Eucharist. The prayer session lasted for about five hours – quite a long healing service – and it was great to be there.

All I can say to describe that fortnight is that it was the beginning of something which I wasn't quite sure of, but certainly it was something that God and Our Lady wanted me to do. It was a whole spiritual renewal, giving me a sense of inner healing and bringing a new direction to my own life regarding Medjugorje, which for me was never going to be the same again. It was a place I had always wanted to go to, but that particular fortnight gave me a good spiritual boost. I had come home spiritually renewed from it; obviously this was to prepare me for what I am still doing today – going to Medjugorje frequently and praying to Our Lady for the conversion of the world. This was to be a great source of comfort, and I no longer dreaded coming back home from Medjugorje because I knew that by living the message, I would always have the spirit of prayer there with me.

So, after spending that fortnight just before the anniversary there, I departed from Medjugorje and returned home, planning to go back that September, which I did. I went back for a week and had one or two other pilgrims with me. The morning that I was due to go back in September, I awoke and thought to myself, 'This will be the last time that I'll be in Medjugorje this year'. No sooner had that thought entered my mind than an inspiration voice told me, 'No it won't, you'll be back there for Christmas'. I left Medjugorje having spent a wonderful week there; the two people with me had never been before and it was also a special time for them.

When I came home that September in 1990, I made up my mind that whatever happened I was going back to Medjugorje for Christmas. A year previous to that I would never have dreamt of going for Christmas, as I lived with my father and I thought it wouldn't be a nice thing to leave him on his own. However, the spirit of God and Our Lady changes these things for better reasons. I prepared as much as I could to return to Medjugorje but had great difficulty trying to get a travel agent to book flights for me, since it was out of season and there were no direct flights going to Dubrovnik or to Split at that time. Then I came into contact with a gentleman in England who referred me to a travel agent who was organising flights from Heathrow to Zagreb and then on to Mostar. I telephoned the travel agent and was told that there was only one seat on the flight and if I wanted it I was to let them know as soon as possible. I had to request time off and this also meant having to request days-in-lieu from the new year's holiday list at work, which I thought I might have difficulty with and possibly not get. However, it turned out that I got the days off work and I booked that last seat to go for Christmas.

As it was the first time I'd ever been across to Heathrow airport on my own, it was an exciting experience. The day came for me to depart; I think it was the 21st December. I was unfamiliar with Heathrow in those days and I had to first of all make my own way from Terminal 1 to Terminal 2 to catch the flight going to Zagreb, and then continue on to Belgrade. When we got off the plane at Zagreb we had to catch an internal flight to Mostar. That evening, fog delayed the flight to Mostar and we thought that we might have to be transferred by bus. This would be an incredibly long journey, about a six hour drive, but it turned out that the fog lifted, enabling the flight to take off an hour or so later than scheduled. I wasn't sure if I had a place to stay or not, but there was a group from England there who brought me on their bus to Medjugorje. The guide, who I've got to know well since, said to me, 'Why don't you stay with this group and you can pay the woman at the end of the week?' So I did.

So it was my first Christmas and winter in Medjugorje. The weather was cold at night and the days were frosty bright and crisp. The house was quite cold as we didn't have central heating, only a Supersir and a gas heater in the dining room. We didn't mind this experience; it was simply a privilege to be there for Christmas. Again full of enthusiasm, I went up around the church area to find that the big church was not being used for the English Mass; it was just the smaller Adoration Church as the crowds were small.

As Christmas approached, the crowds got bigger and so the English Mass moved into the main church. It was the first time Christmas was recognised as a public holiday in Bosnia Herzegovina. The communist authorities hadn't previously allowed it, but this year in 1991 it was a special Christmas, following the Turkish occupation of that country. It was a Christmas filled with joy and enthusiasm for the local people. Unlike our own Christmases, buying presents is not customary in that country.

On the feast of St Nicholas on 7th December the parish of Medjugorje celebrates a great children's Mass where after the Mass one of the priests dresses up as Santa Claus and brings out little gifts, sweets or little hampers, to the village children. Some of the foreign people who now live in Medjugorje have brought their own gift-giving custom with them.

We noticed that Christmas in Medjugorje involved a tremendous amount of fireworks, which are more associated with Halloween here in Ireland. These would be let off around the church area, particularly after the midnight Mass. That first Christmas we had the adoration of the Blessed Sacrament, which began as usual at 10pm, and as the hour went on the church filled up with people, until it was packed to standing room only capacity. The midnight Mass followed; all of this usually lasts until 1 or 1:30 in the morning. This was to me a tremendously holy experience and a wonderful way to spend Christmas.

On Christmas day the local people of Medjugorje gather in the church for their Mass, after which they wish each other happy Christmas and also go out to welcome the pilgrims there as well. Then the local families usually gather in their own homes for lunch, and after that they return to the neighbourhood. The men get together and visit each of the houses on the streets they live in. This usually goes on all afternoon, the men spend about ten or fifteen minutes in each house, wishing the people a happy Christmas and singing Croatian songs, also sipping wine and eating cakes – another custom associated with Christmas in Medjugorje.

As for the pilgrims, we had the normal English Mass at midday, after which we went back to the house where we were staying and had our lunch. The family of the house made us welcome, thanked us for coming to spend Christmas with them, and prayed with us before sitting down for lunch. The Christmas lunch in Medjugorje is slightly different to the usual big Irish spread of turkey and ham. However, having enjoyed their way of life at Christmas, we went to the church for the evening prayer programme, the Rosary at five o'clock and Mass in Croatian at six; that continues 365 days a year. Usually Our Lady does appear on Christmas day, but I will tell you more about this in a later chapter which is devoted to the apparitions.

On our way home, after spending Christmas in Medjugorje in 1990, we encountered some difficulties. When we arrived at Mostar airport at seven o'clock in the morning to catch the flight to Zagreb, we found the airport was fog-bound. This delayed the flight considerably, until about three o'clock in the afternoon, during which time the airline decided they would take us to a local hotel and provide us with lunch. When we returned to the airport later that afternoon, the fog had lifted and the plane had landed so we were ready to take off for Zagreb. However we'd missed our connecting flight to London, so were not able to fly until the following day. Boarded on to a bus we were driven about one hundred miles away to Ljubljana, where our new flight was to depart from. There we were put up in a hotel for the night, and looked after very well. This seemed to some of us like a little reward for making the effort and inconveniencing ourselves by coming to Medjugorje for Christmas. We were given a hot meal and a room for the night, compliments of the airline. The following morning we were flown from Ljubljana to London, where I had missed my connecting flight to Dublin, but managed to get another one.

To me it was a wonderful experience to have spent that Christmas in Medjugorje; in fact the whole year of 1990 was very special in relation to Medjugorje. I will end this chapter by saying, I cannot thank God enough for these apparitions and hope to continue to be able to do so in the future by visiting Medjugorje, but above all by living the message which I have been inspired to live. This chapter should end with the message given on 25th of December, Christmas day 1990:

'Dear children! Today I invite you in a special way to pray for peace. Dear children, without peace you cannot experience the birth of the little Jesus either today or in your daily lives. Therefore, pray to the Lord of Peace, that He may protect you with His mantle and that He may help you to comprehend the greatness and the importance of peace in your heart. In this way you shall be able to spread peace from your heart throughout the whole world. I am with you and I intercede for you before God. Pray, because Satan wants to destroy my plans of peace. Be reconciled with one another and by means of your lives, help peace reign on the whole earth. Thank you for having responded to my call.'

The outbreak of war and travelling to Medjugorje during the war years

On the 26th of June 1981, the third day of the apparitions, on her way down the mountain after having the apparition, Maria Pavolvic was taken to one side. Our Lady appeared to her and behind Our Lady was a black cross. Maria said that Jesus was not on the cross. Our Lady said in Croatian, 'Mir, mir, mir'. She said, 'Peace, peace, peace and only peace! Peace must reign between God and man and among all people!' Ten years later on the 26th June 1991, the war broke out in the former Yugoslavia.

Towards the end of 1990, there were different ethnic groups fighting one another in the southern regions of Yugoslavia. In the independent province of Kosovo and Macedonian Republic, factions were developing. In 1991 I visited Medjugorje at Easter for the first time that year – my first Easter there. There was tension in the air and rumours about the possibility of war, although some of us found it difficult to believe.

When I returned to Medjugorje for the anniversary celebrations in June of that year, the reality became apparent. On the 24th and 25th, people started to gather to celebrate the tenth anniversary of the apparitions. The crowds were exceptionally big, as the anniversary fell on the day before a weekend, which attracted larger crowds from the Croatian republic and also from the republic of Bosnia and Herzegovina. On the 26th of June, word got out that war had been declared in Kosovo and Croatia, when people there had voted for independence from the federation of Yugoslavia, which was against the Serbs' wishes. The Serbs started to attack Kosovo and the war eventually spread to Croatia. It was strange to see Medjugorje deserted. Within twenty-four hours of the outbreak of war the Americans had prepared to leave, the British were also ordered to leave by their embassies and we the Irish discussed the situation with Father Philip, the American priest. We were used to political unrest back home, so simply decided to stay where we were until it was time to go back. That we did and we found it strange that the outbreak of war could bring about the evacuation of most pilgrims from Medjugorje.

That particular week of the anniversary, I was with a group from Northern Ireland and Bernie, a friend of mine from Warrenpoint, was the leader of the group. We stayed in a nice big house just below the Cross Mountain, which was roughly about half an hour's walk from the church. I remember that week quite well; it was a warm week and there was a great atmosphere amongst the group in the house. We didn't mind staying so far away from the church although the heat got to us during the walk. It wasn't so bad going down towards the village but coming back uphill from the church was another matter. There were two nice priests in the group and it meant a prayerful and a spontaneous week as well. We did various things, such as climbing the Apparition Hill, particularly on the night of the 24th of June when there was an apparition. It was the eve of the anniversary and we had the privilege of being in among the crowd of people for the apparition that night.

On the 25th of June, the church itself was overcrowded for the English Mass. An archbishop from the Philippines, who had come from his country with a group, led us in the Mass. During the homily, he spoke about the problems in Baghdad at that particular time – you know bombing by the United Nations and the trouble there. He told us that the United States was understood to be unhappy with the reaction of the Serbs to the declaration of independence by the Federal State of Croatia and the Federal Republic of Kosovo.

On the Saturday morning we prepared to go home. We took the bus up to Split where we were to catch our flight. When we arrived at Split, we could see the obvious signs of war - soldiers and military personnel all over the streets. Although Split itself wasn't under any threat of attack at that stage, further up the road in

Zagreb there had been a few shellings. We boarded the plane and, as we left Split, I wondered how long it would be before I could come back to Medjugorje again. I knew that God and Our Lady had entrusted me with a mission to pray for the conversion of others and particularly to frequent Medjugorje, but when would I be back there?

We landed in Belfast airport that day and I remember bumping into a lady from Donegal called Donna and we spoke for a brief moment. Little did I know that she had been planning her wedding for later that year. I've since become very friendly with herself and her husband. When we got to Belfast we learned that the charter flights to Yugoslavia, Medjugorje, were going to stop because of the war. In fact they didn't resume until the anniversary of 1994. It was in November that year, when I was attending a prayer meeting, that I was shown a picture of a couple who'd got married in October 1991 in Medjugorje and who I knew, it was Donna and her husband Marinko Ostovjić, and I wondered why she got married in a country where the threat of war and violence was looming.

It wasn't until February of '92 that I prepared to go back to Medjugorje again. I had been praying for the grace to return to Medjugorje ever since I had been there for the anniversary of '91. I had wanted to go back in October of that year, but was advised not to by a travel agent friend of mine. I heeded his advice although it was against my own inclinations. I decided to go to Fatima in October '91, which wasn't what I wanted but it was nice to be there all the same.

Just after Christmas in 1992, when we were looking at the news reporting on the war one night, my father said to me, 'You must be due to go back there soon'. I was already planning a trip there but had been afraid to tell him. This was his way of finding out! I told him that I was hoping to go back the following month, February. A few days later I won a prize of £1000 in the parish draw. I knew the trip would be more expensive than usual so this was the answer to my prayer; I should return to Medjugorje with the money I had won. So I rang my travel agent friend in Dublin and mentioned the idea of going back to Medjugorje. He informed me that there was a ceasefire on so it might an ideal time to go back and see what the story was. He was hoping to resume the charter flights that summer but would have to wait and see what was happening – there was an air of uncertainty about the whole situation.

So I booked the flights and headed off on 13th of February that year. We left Newry for Dublin airport, my friend Tom the travel agent met me there with the tickets and wished me all the best. I flew to Belgrade via Heathrow on my own, and from there I took an internal flight to Sarajevo. When we arrived at Sarajevo it was quite late, about eight o'clock in the evening. My first impression at that time was that it was a bit threatening, so I decided that the best thing to do was to keep on going and get to Medjugorje that night. When I came through the customs at Sarajevo airport I asked a taxi driver where I could get transport to Medjugorje. He took me over to a bus information counter and the lady said there was a bus at eleven o'clock that night. However, the taxi driver told me that his friend, who was also a taxi driver, was taking someone to Mostar, and he would be willing to take me on to Medjugorje. We agreed, so I got into a taxi. Despite exchanging words in different languages, we agreed a price of about sixty pounds sterling for the taxi ride, which is about one hundred miles.

On the way he dropped his friend in Mostar, and then we proceeded through the mountains to Medjugorje. During the journey, we were stopped on three occasions at different checkpoints. I didn't know whether these checkpoints were manned by Serbs or Croatians. On the third occasion that we were stopped, I was asked for my passport and the police came to my side of the car, opened the door and requested that I get out. At this point I have to say that I was afraid what might happen because I didn't know what type of policeman he was. My heart was

in my mouth, as I thought I was going to be shot. He
asked me to open my bag, which was in the boot, and
I did so. He searched the bag, asked me to close it
again and then he flicked through my passport for a
few minutes. As he was doing that, an inner voice
said to me, 'Just hold on Patrick, just relax, this is not
the RUC or the British army you're facing here, just
relax'. So with that he gave me back the passport and
told me to go back into the car again and they let us
through.

When I got to Medjugorje I could find nowhere to
stay. It was about one o'clock in the morning and,
after a recommendation from one of the local people,
the driver decided to take me back to a hotel in Ljuti
Dolac, about five miles outside Medjugorje. The
following morning I got a taxi into Medjugorje itself,
where he dropped me at the church. It was completely
deserted, so I sat outside the church and wondered
what to do. I'd come here, there was no one about and
I'd nowhere to stay. I decided to go into the church
and I put my bag on the seat. I knelt down and said to
Our Lady, 'Blessed Lady you've brought me here
now, I've nowhere to go and nowhere to stay and
there's nobody here. I'm going to pray this Rosary
and ask you to help me to find somewhere to stay or
to guide me as to what I should do'. So with that I
started to pray the Rosary, and at the last prayer a
lady tapped me on the shoulder. She was an Irish lady

and she said, 'You're very welcome but what are you doing here and how did you get here? Where are you staying?' I said that first of all I was praying for somebody to help me because I had just arrived that morning had nowhere to stay. She asked how long I was staying, I replied, 'I'm here for a week, I hope, but I still don't know whether to stay or not.' However she said that I could come and stay in her mother-in-law's house if I liked. It was Donna, the friend whose picture I had seen on the cover of the magazine that November when she got married. She and her husband were going to the English Mass which was being celebrated in the little apparition chapel just beside the altar of the main church. They had gone in but Donna came back out and said that if I wanted to I could come in for Mass in English; that it would be starting shortly and then afterwards maybe we could go and have a cup of coffee and talk.

When I went into the Mass the American priest, Father Philip, recognised me and he came over and shook my hand. He said 'You're very welcome and you're very brave for coming here, how did you get here?' So we exchanged a few words about how I got there and he said, 'Well I'm delighted you've come here'. I suppose it was good for them to know that people were still thinking of them. So after Mass I went for a cup of coffee with Donna and her husband, the newly married couple. After coffee we walked through the fields over to her mother-in-law's house, which was beside their own new house. There her mother-in-law Jela and her father-in-law Ivan welcomed me into their home and, since their other son was out serving in the army, they gave me his room to stay in for the week.

That day in the afternoon, having had a rest, I climbed the Apparition Hill with the parishioners of Medjugorje who, every Sunday afternoon during the war, said the Rosary while climbing the hill; they still do that today. It was that evening, after having a meal with Donna's parents-in-law, that Donna invited me to and her husband's house, where I could have a conversation with somebody in English. So myself and Donna got acquainted then. I had known Donna prior to this, as she had been a guide in Medjugorje for a couple of years and I'd stayed in the same house as her. So we had a good week that week.

The following morning we went to the English Mass, which was held again in the little apparition chapel off the main altar. After this we went for a coffee; Donna and I became good companions that week. We also went up the Apparition Hill and on the second or third day of the week, Donna took me over to meet one of the visionaries – Vicka Ivankovic. There were also a few other pilgrims from America there, so we had a few reflections from Vicka, and then she prayed over us and invited us to pray together.

During that week I walked through the fields on a number of occasions over to the base of the Apparition Hill, and saw the farmers planting seed for the new grape in the vineyard, and all the work that was going on. Something convinced me that week – even though there was a threat of war on Bosnia and Herzegovina just around the corner – that Our Lady would protect Medjugorje. Something convinced me that even though the war did come to the doorstep of this place, it was not going to destroy it. There was a threat issued that the Serbs were going to bomb Medjugorje; that they wanted to bomb St James' church and the Cross Mountain. During that week I remember sitting with Ivan and Jela and quite often they would be listening to the news on radio or television. It became apparent that week that Bosnia and Herzegovina would vote for independence, which had been ratified by the United Nations.

Then it was my time to go home, having spent a peaceful and welcome week in Medjugorje; I'd had a strong desire to go back there since June the previous year. I was leaving Medjugorje quite early to catch a flight from Sarajevo. Towards the end of the week I had asked Donna about arranging a taxi to take me to the airport. However, Marinko volunteered to drive me and Donna decided that he wasn't going on his own, that she would accompany him. So very early on the Saturday morning, we set off for Sarajevo. Ivan was a bit apprehensive but Marinko insisted that he would be ok. We drove down through Mostar and headed out towards the mountains. We were climbing one of the main mountains when we came across some freezing fog and snow and ice. As we climbed the mountain the temperature descended to minus five. We ended up in a situation where the car could go no further; the frost and the snow were preventing it from climbing the hill, so we drove back down to a garage in a little village at the bottom of the hill called Konjic. There, Marinko purchased some snow chains and we drove up the hill again and into Sarajevo. During that part of the journey, I remember asking Marinko if he thought the flight would go on time. He said that it may be delayed because of the weather, which would be good.

When we arrived at Sarajevo airport, I went to check in, but I was told that the flight had gone on time. The airline was called JAT, they were the Yugoslav airline at the time and their nickname was 'Joke About Time' – but they weren't joking about it this time! They had left Sarajevo on time on that snowy morning. We were told to go to the customer service desk, but when we got there the lady abruptly said, 'You have missed the flight, you have got to buy a new ticket and the ticket will cost you £300'. This I thought was a bit much and it was hard to take in, so we decided we would go up to the restaurant and have a cup of coffee and work out what we were going to do. We were sitting talking when Marinko decided that we would take a drive into Sarajevo to his friend's apartment. From there, Marinko made a phone call to the Chief of Police, who had been a university companion of his, and explained my predicament to him. The Chief of Police then contacted the chief of the airline of Sarajevo and I was instructed to be at JAT's office in the city centre at about two o'clock that afternoon.

That morning we walked around Sarajevo, which was full of snow and our feet were really cold. When we met the Chief of Police, he brought us in and bought us something to eat; he was a nice gentleman. He told us that he'd had a word with his senior counterpart in the airline and he felt that she would be able to fix me up. So in the afternoon, we went back to JAT's office and the lady herself came to me and told me that I wouldn't have to purchase another ticket, that I would be issued with a new one, and that I would fly to Belgrade that night, stay in the Hotel Belgrade and would fly on to London the following morning, which I did.

One week after I left Sarajevo, the bombing and

shelling started. I remember ringing Donna and on one occasion, she said to me, 'You were very lucky you got away when you did'. The bombing of Sarajevo lasted for a number of months and as most people are aware, the bombing of Srebrenica also. Our television screens were full of sad stories. The war began in Mostar and it was becoming nearly impossible to travel in that region. The phone lines were cut off and we were not able to contact anybody for about two to three months. I remember one day at work, I think it was at the end of April or the beginning of May, an inspiration gave me a little hope, saying, 'You will see your friends soon'.

Shortly after that, the manager came along to me at work and asked me if I was taking any holidays, I said I was contemplating going to Medjugorje and he said, 'You're what? You're not going out there?!' I told him I was undecided and was waiting for a lady to come back from the region and let me know what the state of affairs was, as she'd travelled to see her daughter there. He said, 'Right... well anyway if you're taking holidays let me know and tell the administration desk as well.' So, having contacted Donna's mother and been told that the situation in Medjugorje was calm at that moment, I decided to go myself. She said that she had felt quite safe there, but advised us to go the way that she had; from London to Zagreb and from there take a flight to Split.

So I contacted a friend in a travel agency in Dublin. He had another friend living in Dublin who wanted to go out there for humanitarian purposes. I told her the story and advised her that I would be travelling. There were other people from my own area who travelled with me: the late Carmel Smith, Patrick McCreesh and Bernie O'Hare. We prepared to leave for Medjugorje, although at the same time our families thought we were a bit nuts! Nevertheless, we booked a flight and decided to go on Saturday 20th of June for the anniversary, to stay in Medjugorje for at least ten days. We left our homes on the Saturday and headed towards Dublin airport to meet the rest of the group, there were I think twelve people in total. We flew from Dublin over to Heathrow, where we collected our bags to check in for the flight to Zagreb with the new Croatia Airlines which left from terminal two. However, at the reclaim baggage area, Carmel unfortunately lifted the wrong bag by mistake, and no one realised until we got to Zagreb.

When we arrived at Zagreb, we had to take another flight to Split. Before we could board this flight, we were asked to identify our bags, and this is when we discovered that Carmel had taken the wrong one. However, she had to take the wrong bag on with her to Medjugorje, since there wasn't much the airline could do about it. We arrived in Split at about six o'clock that evening and headed for a nearby hotel where we were to spend the night. It was amazing to find life as normal in Split; the war in Croatia had ceased and people were getting on with life. The hotel made us welcome and we had a nice meal and a bit of refreshment. We were able to take a walk into the centre of the town and relax and enjoy the evening.

The following morning after breakfast, we headed through the old city of Split and we had Mass in the church there. When we arrived back at the hotel, the minibus that was to take us to Medjugorje was waiting there. We were getting our bags from the hotel and Sean, a Galway man who was travelling on the bus, was anxious to get away. As I was the person responsible for organising the bus, he told me in a strong Galway accent, 'Never mind those women Patrick; get that bus on the road and let's get on our way up to Medjugorje!' I was as anxious to get away as he was, and eventually we got everybody on board and headed out through the city of Split and onto the road, down the coast and up into Medjugorje.

As we approached the boarder of Croatia, which leads into Bosnia Herzegovina, the only sign of war was that we were asked for our passports. Then we drove straight through and arrived at our destination, our house, at about two o'clock in the afternoon. Patsy, Carmel, Bernie and myself were staying with my friend Donna, who I'd met the February before and had since become part of their family to a certain extent. They welcomed us into their home. Until the previous night there had been no electricity, and still no running water. About an hour or so after we arrived, we were having a cup of tea after the water came back on. This was a great relief to us all, especially to Donna, who was able to resume some sort of a normal life again.

Later we went down for the evening prayer programme. Until the Thursday prior to that, the church had been closed for fear of shelling and bombing. As it was the feast of Corpus Christi, the parish priest, Father Ivan Landeka, decided that the church should be reopened and the Blessed Sacrament resumed in the Tabernacle. This was at an appropriate time, in preparation for the anniversary. When we arrived down at the church area, the local priests were full of emotion to see foreigners arriving back to their village. It signified a return to normality was approaching. So we went in for the Rosary, Croatian Mass and the evening programme. After that, we headed back through the fields to our accommodation at Donna's house, where we had a nice warm meal, a bit of a chat and a few glasses of wine. Donna filled us in about the various events over the last two or three months, shelling of surrounding areas, and airplanes coming close, trying to bomb the village. She told us that she herself was nearly a victim of it, but thankfully they were all protected. I have no doubt that the prayers of the local people helped to protect Medjugorje. A story had come out that a pilot from Serbia, who had been instructed to go to Medjugorje and to carry out bombing there, was blinded by a light and had to turn back. He flew to Split, where he surrendered to the Croatians and told them his story. I believe that he has since converted to Catholicism.

During that week a number of other foreigners started to arrive, which brought a great sense of joy to the local people and priests, and on the 24th of June they decided to hold a peace march from the nearby parish of Ljubuški. From there a number of people walked the seven miles into Medjugorje, led by the Blessed Sacrament, and the priests called for an end to the war. It wasn't until about four years later that the war finally ended. That night on the Apparition Hill, we attended an apparition and there was quite a crowd of people there. During the apparition, Our Lady urged us to pray during these troubled times.

We were there for about ten days and one evening, we had the privilege of attending the apparition in the church. It was held on the balcony of the choir loft. Ivan, the visionary, was going up to the apparition, with Father Slavko following, we asked if we could also go up, and they obliged us. I think we were the only foreigners in the village at that time; it was shortly after the anniversary. We went up for the Rosary which began at six o'clock and then there was a pause for the apparition at about twenty minutes to seven. We were behind Ivan, and all I can really say is that it was as if the eyes of my soul were able to see Our Lady. My physical eyes weren't able to see her, but I felt her presence. After the apparition we shook hands with Ivan and thanked him for permitting us to be present with him on the balcony.

We continued with the evening programme and then went back to Donna's house, where we had our evening meal and a bit of craic with Donna and her husband. Donna remarked that we were full of enthusiasm and joy, and when I explained we'd just been at the apparition, she said, 'Well you must have got something out of it'. It did fill us with joy, and I think it was a little reward from Our Lady for the efforts we'd made to travel to Medjugorje on that occasion.

The time to go came fairly quickly. We left Medjugorje quite early, at about four o'clock in the morning, and drove again through the country, down to Split where we were to board our flight to Zagreb. As we were checking in it turned out that the flight was overbooked. For the airline, which hadn't been in business very long, this situation was an embarrassment. However we were able to get on to the flight to London. We arrived back in Heathrow and got a connecting flight to Dublin. By the time we got home we were tired but there was a great sense of purpose, achievement and faith, to have made that particular pilgrimage in 1992. Coming from a troubled part of the world, we had found ourselves in an even worse situation during our time there. We had even heard the bombing and the shelling in Mostar, about twenty miles away.

Quite often, day and night we had heard the sounds of the brutality that was going on, yet in Medjugorje we were in a totally peaceful area. I believed that Medjugorje itself and the prayers of the people there, helped to preserve the peace within the village and protect its people, allowing life to go on as normally as possible, particularly at the shrine itself, where people were free to come and pray. A member of our group, Kay Vary, who was involved with humanitarian work following the pilgrimage, visited areas affected by the war and was disturbed at some of the sights. Quite frequently there were power cuts, and if we wanted to go out around the village at night, we had to do so in complete darkness; we weren't even allowed to shine a torch. This was to deter any shelling over the village during the night.

When I got home after that first visit at the height of the war, I was as always anxious to return. My next visit was unexpected and very soon afterwards. One Sunday afternoon in my room, my mind was focused on the Apparition Hill. Suddenly, I had an inspiration to return to Medjugorje. Within a fortnight from that Sunday I was actually on the hill.

My next visit was on the 15th of August that year. I left Dublin on the same journey I'd made six weeks prior to that. A gentleman from Limerick joined me there in Donna's house. Donna had a routine of climbing the Apparition Hill and praying the Rosary and the following day, the Sunday afternoon, she suggested that I join her, so Donna helped me walk up the hill. Halfway up, there's a cross marking the spot where Our Lady appeared to Maria the visionary on the 26th of June and gave her the message about peace and only peace. We stopped there for a while; said a prayer and sang the hymn Our Lady of Knock. Then we proceeded with our climb to the site of the apparition itself. There we stayed in silent prayer for a few moments, and despite the noise going on in the distance in Mostar, there was a tremendous sense of peace and security there. We headed back down to the base of the hill where we continued our walk through the fields. We struck up a very good friendship during that visit as well.

One of the highlights of that visit was when one afternoon, Donna, myself and the other gentleman from Limerick took a trip down to the nearby town of Capljina, which had been shelled during the bombing. This was about ten miles from Medjugorje, just on the border. So we drove down to see the wreckage of the town and found it deserted - bullet-holed buildings, glass all over the footpath from broken windows, and quiet, with nobody about. This town had been bombed in March of that year and had remained empty ever since, so many people had fled to safety. The bridge over the river Neretva, which flows from Mostar down into the sea, had been shelled too. I have never seen so much destruction in all my life; had never seen a town brought to its knees, even though I came from a troubled area. The sight saddened me. Having said that, now Capljina has fully recovered from the war, people are living there again and a new bridge has been built so traffic is flowing freely again – life goes on! However the scars of war are still there to this day.

I returned home after that visit having spent a week there, and once again I wondered, because of the war, when I would be able to go back again. I continued to pray for the grace to return there because it required both grace and faith. Each time I was fearful of what might happen, particularly during that year.

During lunchtime at work, I had a regular habit of visiting the Cathedral across the road to pray the

Rosary. One afternoon at the end of November I went there as usual. I had started into the first decade of the Rosary when an inner voice said to me, 'You will go to Medjugorje for Christmas; you will take two days out of next year's leave'. The voice inspired me to do this, so I finished my prayers and went back to work for the afternoon. I enquired about the possibility of being able to take two days from the following year's leave so that I could go for Christmas '92. This request was granted to me and I booked the flights to go. As soon as I had done so I felt everything had fallen into place. It was as if Our Lady had invited me to come once again, this time for Christmas.

I arrived on the 20th of December, back into the home of my friends Donna and Marinko, where I spent Christmas with them and their family. That Christmas is one I will always remember. The midnight Mass and adoration went ahead, although they were not publicised. There were not many pilgrims about, but it was very special to spend Christmas with one of the local families. They made me very welcome, and when I left and returned home, it was then that I appreciated the visit and the great graces that had been given to me there. My urge was to go back and again this happened sooner rather than later, and I headed back that February '93. I boarded a flight, headed for London and once again landed at Zagreb to board a connecting flight on to Split.

The unusual thing about this flight was that when the aircraft was about to take off, one of the engines blew. The pilot managed to bring the aircraft to a stop and return it to the ramp. We were told that the aircraft itself was out of commission, that it had technical difficulties. We had to disembark and our next flight didn't take off until about three hours later. Eventually we arrived at Split around ten o'clock that night and Donna's husband Marinko was there to meet me. This was one year after the incident in Sarajevo. He drove me from Split airport, home to Medjugorje in good time; we arrived at roughly about midnight. The phones were down so Marinko was not able to call Donna; she didn't know anything about our whereabouts and was quite anxious when we arrived so late. I explained about the aircraft's difficulty. Incidents like these can be frightening, but as I'm a frequent flyer I took it as one of those things; I didn't let it frighten me.

During that week in February '93 there were the visionaries and various events, the Masses and the evening prayer programme. I also visited Medjugorje at Easter that year for the anniversary, and again at the end of August, when I took two friends from my own area, who had never been before. They themselves were deeply moved by the whole situation with the war. In November '93, I again found myself inspired to go back to Medjugorje for a week and was able to do so. I found that these inspirations were necessary; the prayer was necessary during that time when there was so much hatred and destruction of human life, and war was being waged in that country.

It wasn't until many years later that I pondered the question - why was I being called there so often? Quite early one morning I was preparing to return to Medjugorje for Christmas. I remember asking myself, why do I go there every Christmas and why am I being called? A strange peace came over me and an inspiration, which I have no doubt was Our Lady, said to me, 'It is because so few people are willing'. I understood that it is due to the will to pray, the desire to inconvenience and sacrifice oneself for others. The call that I receive to Medjugorje continues today. I went many times during the war and eventually the war came to an end in 1995.

This chapter should end with the messages of 25th of June '92, and a message given in 1994, when Our Lady thanked the people for praying for the end of the war. That gave great hope to a people who had suffered so much. It turned out that Mostar itself had suffered great and terrible losses. The division between ethnic groups in Mostar caused the break-up of families and homes. One has to ask the question, could the war have been avoided? It's hard to know. I have no doubt that if enough people respond to Our

Lady's call, war can be averted. Our Lady tells us in the messages that by prayer and fasting you can suspend natural laws and even stop wars.

Medjugorje Message, June 25, 1992

'Dear children! Today I am happy, even if in my heart there is still a little sadness for all those who have started on this path and then left it. My presence here is to take you on a new path, the path to salvation. This is why I call you, day after day, to conversion. But if you do not pray, you cannot say that you are on the way to being converted. I pray for you and I intercede to God for peace; first peace in your hearts and also peace around you, so that God may be your peace. Thank you for having responded to my call.'

Medjugorje Message, February 25, 1994

'Dear children! Today I thank you for your prayers. All of you have helped me so that this war may end as soon as possible. I am close to you and I pray for each one of you and I beg you: pray, pray, pray. Only through prayer can we defeat evil and protect all that Satan wants to destroy in your lives. I am your Mother and I love you all equally, and I intercede for you before God. Thank you for having responded to my call.'

The all-night vigils at Mount Melleray Grotto sow the seeds for pilgrimages to Medjugorje

For hundreds of years, Mount Melleray has been known as a centre of monastic life. The Cistercian monks have been based there for quite some time. It was in 1980 that one of the monks of the monastery erected a grotto, about a mile or two from the monastery, dedicated to Our Lady of Lourdes.

In August 1985, three young children; Barry, Ursula and Tom, said that Our Lady had appeared to them while they were visiting the grotto. They said that she appeared to them for nine days in succession, speaking to them and teaching them how to pray the Rosary. Word spread around Cappoquin and the surrounding districts, attracting crowds of people. During the time that Our Lady is said to have been appearing at the grotto at Melleray, she showed them three apocalyptic visions: first, Noah's Ark; second, doubting Thomas; third, the desecration of churches. The children did not understand these visions at the time, but, as it turned out about twenty five years later, they were warnings of times to come in the Catholic Church in Ireland.

The story of Noah's Ark signified the purification that the church would have to undergo, and those who were consecrated to Our Lady, who is the Ark of the new Covenant, would be protected in their faith. The story of doubting Thomas signified that there were many believers and unbelievers in the Church, both laity and clergy, and as a consequence of the purification of the church, many would fall away from their faith. In the third sequence, Our Lady showed them property being removed from the Church and the Church being destroyed. There were a lot of rotten apples within the Church who would have to be removed before it could be reconstructed in Ireland. This is now not only happening in Ireland, but all over the world.

Within ten years of those reported events at Melleray Grotto, the Church scandals began to emerge and they are still emerging today. I heard about these events shortly after they had happened, but didn't take much interest in them, as I believed in the apparitions of Medjugorje. I didn't see the sense of Our Lady having to come to Ireland to point out these situations, however now I see the reason for that.

In spring 1991, a friend of mine contacted me one day, saying that she had a group going to Mount Melleray the following day for an all-night vigil, and would I like to join her. As it was a bank holiday weekend, I decided I would join her group. The buses would leave in the afternoon and arrive at Melleray in time for the vigil. We stayed up all night praying in the Grotto, after which we headed to early Mass at seven o'clock, then had breakfast and journeyed back home again. It was a tiring pilgrimage, but one of great sacrifice however.

The same friend contacted me later that year in November, and asked whether I could join her for another pilgrimage to Mount Melleray. In Newry we boarded a bus, which had come from the Dungannon area, and headed towards Melleray Grotto. On the journey down to Melleray, it is customary to pray the Rosary. On this occasion, it was being led by one of the passengers, and we responded enthusiastically. After the first Rosary on this particular journey, we sang a hymn, and after the praying and the singing finished, one of the women on the bus said, 'There is a man down here who is a good singer' - she was referring to me. She added, 'He would I'm sure be willing to sing a few hymns', and I was glad to oblige. They asked me if I would like to lead the remainder of the Rosary, and I said that I would. During the course of the journey, the organiser of the bus trip asked for my name. I told her, 'My name is Patrick McGrath'. She said, 'Before you got on the bus, your name came into my head', and I said, 'Well, probably because it was on the list', and she said,

'No, I didn't look at the list, but your name came into my head'. So that night, I led them in prayer in the grotto, and a number of people reported having various manifestations. It has been claimed that people have visions at the grotto; that the statue of Our Lady at the grotto comes to life! I don't pay much attention to these claims, they may or may not happen, I don't know. However, the important thing is that people went there to pray and they stayed up all night, even in the coldness of winter.

About a fortnight later, I had a phone call at my place of work; it was the lady who had organised the bus trip a couple of weeks before. She said there was another bus going down to Melleray, and that she'd tried to look for my number and that this was the first bank that she'd rung. She asked if I would be interested in coming, because she needed somebody to lead the prayer. I said, 'Fine I'll certainly come'. So from December '91 until August '95, we had buses going to Mount Melleray. I was responsible for leading the prayer on the bus, and in the grotto as well. It was also an opportunity for me to talk about Medjugorje and explain the messages, while I had the microphone. Many of those who did not know about Medjugorje became aware of the messages then.

In March '94, on our way down to Mount Melleray, we had stopped for something to eat, and I had the following idea. I told Bernie, who was sitting in front of me, 'I would like you, Bernie, to help me to run a pilgrimage to Medjugorje later this year'. She agreed, and told her other friend. By the time we boarded the bus again to continue our journey to Mount Melleray, there were twenty-four people who said they would like to go. They did go, along with about nine or ten others. On June 20th of that year there was a Mass in Dublin airport, to mark the resumption of direct flights and pilgrimages to Medjugorje, since they had stopped in 1991 when the war had started. This I attended with another friend and it was a nice experience to celebrate that it would no longer be necessary to go to Heathrow to get to Medjugorje – at least during the summer anyway.

On September 23rd of that year, the first pilgrimage of those people who travelled on the bus to Mount Melleray left for Medjugorje. We spent one week there on pilgrimage, and for many of those people it was the first time they had been there. As a consequence of that, every year in September, until more or less the present year, myself and Bernadette Kennedy, who was from Dungannon, organised a group pilgrimage from both our local areas. In the early years, '95 to '98, the numbers grew, and people who had come on pilgrimage with us, took their own groups to Medjugorje. I have no doubt that the Holy Spirit, when inspiring me to ask Bernadette to help to organise the pilgrimage, had a great plan in mind. As a result of that first pilgrimage in '94, hundreds of people have visited Medjugorje, and hundreds are continuing to do so, and to bring other people there.

In June '98 and again in September '98, Bernadette Kennedy, myself and Patsy McCreesh, organised two groups. On the latter occasion, the extra incentive for the pilgrimage was the visit of the Holy Father Pope John Paul II to the city of Split. For that visit, a number of busses left Medjugorje to join the pilgrims for the Holy Father's Mass, on the coast at Split. The morning in question was a Sunday morning; we arose quite early and left at about 3am. However, because there were more buses than anticipated, the journey was delayed for about an hour. When we eventually arrived in Split, at about six o'clock in the morning, we disembarked from the bus and made our way down to the sea shore, where the Holy Father's Mass was going to take place. It was a very special occasion and a lot of people from the parish of Medjugorje were there to participate in that Mass.

The Holy Father had not been able to visit Medjugorje, so Medjugorje itself came to him. The Mass was celebrated with several other priests and bishops. This was the first time that I had noticed in the Holy Father's voice, the strain of his Parkinson's disease, which was to bring about his death several years later. It was a privilege to be able to make that trip and be with a number of other pilgrims as group leader for that occasion.

Since then we have continued to organise one pilgrimage per year in September, and for almost every pilgrimage, we welcome approximately ten new people. The work of these pilgrimages still goes on, and many people go to Medjugorje and experience the peace and the prayerful atmosphere there; they go home refreshed but also with the desire to return again. Every year the same people come back, bringing with them one or two people who have never been there before. This is important because, from these groups, other groups are generated, which also leads to the conversion of others. There is no doubt that the prayers of people like myself and others who go to Medjugorje, and who try to live the messages daily in their lives at home as well, are helping to bring about these conversions.

The three point break in Bosnia and the cross of sickness

This chapter should begin with the message given in the early years by Our Lady about accepting crosses of sickness and poor health, not as a curse but as a grace, and to pray for the strength to cope with them.

Medjugorje Message, September 11, 1986
'Dear children! For these days while you are joyfully celebrating the cross, I desire that your cross also would be a joy for you. Especially, dear children, pray that you may be able to accept sickness and suffering with love the way Jesus accepted them. Only that way shall I be able with joy to give out to you the graces and healings which Jesus is permitting me. Thank you for having responded to my call.'

In April 1997 I contacted Croatia Airlines and booked a flight from Heathrow to Split for the anniversary later in June. My intention was to stay in Medjugorje for a fortnight. I set off on the pilgrimage on Saturday the 21st of June and arrived early that Sunday morning. For the first couple of days it was the normal routine: attending the English Mass, meeting up with friends and going to the evening prayer programme and other events associated with the pilgrimage, like climbing the Apparition Hill, although the weather at that particular time of the year is extremely warm.

On Tuesday 24th of June, because it was the eve of the anniversary, there was Adoration outside at the main altar. After my evening meal, I decided to leave the place where I was staying and go down to participate in the Adoration. When I arrived outside the main doors of the church, a thought came into my head just to stay where I was and not go down further to the gravel in front of the main altar. However, I ignored the thought and made my way down there. When I thought I was at the bottom of the slope which leads to the gravel, I turned right and without realising, I went over the wall. I fell and broke the top of my hip – the femur. A number of people gathered round to try to assist me, but I was unable to get back up onto my feet. I realised when I heard the crack on falling that I had dislocated or broken something. Two people who knew me were there and they tried to help in their own way, but I asked them to bring my friends Donna and Marinko. They called an ambulance and at the same time Marinko arrived to see what the commotion was about. It turned out that there was a doctor on the scene who, after a quick examination, said that he thought that I had probably broken the bone.

They placed me in the back of the ambulance and Marinko got in with me and said that I would have to go to the nearby clinic to be assessed and see what the situation was. So we proceeded in the ambulance to a clinic in Čitluk, which is about four or five miles away. When we got to the clinic they told us that they didn't have x-ray equipment and that I would have to go to the hospital in Mostar. So we proceeded onwards in the ambulance, down the mountain. Arriving there, it resembled the old hospital that I knew about thirty or forty years ago in my own town of Newry. Some of the doors were too narrow for the stretcher. However, in the end they managed to get a couple of the double-doors open and get it through.

When I was brought into the casualty room the doctor instructed that I should be taken for an x-ray, which revealed that I had broken the hip bone in three places and that I required surgery. I thought I was insured but it turned out I wasn't so I wasn't able to have the surgery in that country, as it would have cost too much money. Marinko decided that it would be better to allow them to plaster the leg; he then brought me back up to his house where I was staying and where I could lie down. It was quite painful when they plastered my leg. On the journey back up to Medjugorje the pain was excruciating as they turned the corners on the drive up through the mountains. When I arrived back at the house, the ambulance man and Marinko lifted me up into my room, where I lay for around a week. They made arrangements for me to be brought home the following Tuesday.

The next morning my family was contacted and my father was informed of what had happened, which caused deep shock and sadness for those back home. The people of Medjugorje reassured them that I was getting the best care possible. Arrangements were made by the Marian Pilgrimage's guide (Philip Brian at the time) that I would be cared for by a nurse, and he himself helped to care for me as well during that week. The day after the accident he visited me and noticed that I was going into a spasm of pain. He said that he had some anti-spasm tablets that I could have and that he would be able to get some more on prescription. These were a great help, as they allowed the muscles to relax, reducing my pain and discomfort. Also, Philip employed a nurse whose name was Mary. She looked after me throughout the week that I was there. Philip was a great help; as I was flat on my back, he came in and gave me a bed bath and washed me down on a couple of occasions. The heat was intense that week and both Philip and Mary tried to make my life there as comfortable as possible.

Soon it was the first of July, which was the day of my departure from Medjugorje. I had arranged that an ambulance would take me to the airport at Split and from there I would be brought on board the chartered flight and placed on three seats at the front for my journey home. Mary the nurse accompanied me home on the aircraft. We left in the ambulance around mid-afternoon and drove for roughly three hours to Split. We arrived at Split airport in good time for the flight. They had arranged that I would be brought through in the ambulance to the air apron where I would be placed in an air ambulance vehicle which would take me to the aircraft.

First of all, they brought me to the paramedics' room and placed me on a bed while the firemen at the airport prepared the narrow stretcher that was to carry me on to the airplane. They eventually placed me on to this stretcher and brought me out to the rear of the aircraft – it was quite hot and the sun was beaming down on my face. I was there for at least ten or fifteen minutes before they could make up their minds whether to bring me in via the front or back door. Finally they placed me on one of the cargo trucks which had a lift on it and hoisted me up into the back of the aircraft.

There were six firemen, so I must have been a heavy person to carry. When I got into the aircraft, the stewardess instructed them to bring me to the front, so the firemen carried me the whole length of the cabin and placed me in the second row of three seats. The chief air-stewardess was concerned about the fact that my leg hadn't been strapped up; they made me as comfortable as they could for the journey however. The airline was an Irish airline – Transair – which has since gone into liquidation, but they did provide a great service for the short number of years that they ferried the pilgrims to Medjugorje and back again.

The rest of the passengers eventually got on board and I was in the unusual position of lying across three seats with my head propped up near the window. The stewardesses strapped me in so that I would be comfortable for take-off and landing. When everybody was on board, the pilot said over the radio that we were about to depart and that it was going to be a little bit uncomfortable for me; I found it all a bit unusual. So we took off from the airport at Split and headed across to Dublin. As we approached Dublin airport down through the clouds, I could see out the window and it was raining. We landed at Dublin at roughly about quarter past ten at night. When we arrived at the terminal building, they got the ramp over to the plane so that the passengers could get off.

When everybody had vacated the aircraft, the St John's ambulance, which I had ordered from Newry, came and arranged that I be lifted off the aircraft. One of the ambulance personnel asked what had happened to me and I told him all about it, after which he ordered his colleague to take out equipment that would make the journey to Newry more comfortable for me. Firstly, they strapped my leg up and then lifted me off the three seats onto a narrow step stretcher. They carried me off the plane and down the corridor to the lift, which they thought was open but turned out to be locked. They decided to carry me down the fire escape beside the aircraft; my two sisters were waiting for me there and were glad to see me. As we entered the terminal building, my father tapped me on the shoulder to reassure me that he was also there.

They put me into the back of the ambulance and made me comfortable for the journey, and my father and two sisters said that they would meet me at the other end. We set off into the wet night, heading for Newry. When I got to Daisy Hill hospital, I was wheeled into casualty and the doctor and nurses attended to me. It was decided, after having taken an x-ray of the leg, that I would be transferred to City Hospital in Belfast where the necessary procedure to correct the break in my leg would be carried out. This was arranged and I was told I would be leaving the next morning. That night in Daisy Hill was a sleepless night, I was quite concerned about the day ahead and the operation that was to follow.

Quite early in the morning the ambulance crew came

and took me off to Belfast City Hospital, where after a short period I was admitted and within an hour, heading for the operating theatre. When I got to the theatre the anaesthetist asked me what exactly had happened and where, and I explained to him that I had been in Medjugorje and had fallen over a wall accidentally. He seemed to have some knowledge of Medjugorje because he said to me, 'That's the place where the pilgrims go', and I said, 'That's correct'. The operation was carried out and in the space of two hours I was in the recovery room and then back on the ward. I was happy that the operation was over and had been a complete success. However, I was not able to put any weight on the leg until about eight weeks later, so that meant a period of time at home recovering.

Those weeks of recovery were long and sometimes quite stressful. I often longed to be able to walk out the door and go back to work again. However the time did pass, slowly but surely. There were sleepless nights sometimes; with that type of break it's often painful and when you're lying down it can be quite uncomfortable. But as time passed by, the pain lessened, the leg began to heal and I was soon able to walk again - on crutches.

After four months I was able to return to work and continued to make a fairly good recovery. Around that time it was suggested one day by a nurse attending to me, that I should consider getting a white cane, advising that after recovering from such a break I would be very vulnerable. After a few days back at work, I decided to take a walk down the street. I saw three gentlemen approach me; I couldn't see from the left side and one of them banged into me. I grabbed a pole nearby which saved me from falling on the exact spot where I had broken my hip. That was a clear indication to me to take seriously the business of getting the white cane. So I contacted the local social services and ordered one, which I have used ever since. I find this to be a great source of protection and find people to be courteous towards me and my disability. I made a full recovery from the broken hip; it took about six to seven months to do so. However, by the end of that year, while many of us were looking forward to entering a new millennium, another cross of suffering and sickness was to come my way.

At the end of 1999, I was preparing to go to Medjugorje on 1st Jan of the year 2000. About two days before, I took what I thought was a stomach bug and brushed it off, thinking it would be gone in forty-eight hours. I went to Medjugorje and during that whole week I was troubled with it. I remember ringing a friend on a couple of occasions during the week saying that I still had this, what I thought was a stomach bug. I came back home on the 8th of January and made an appointment to see my local GP, who encouraged me to continue taking Imodium tablets as it was a bout of diarrhoea. I didn't get any better and after having been at home for over a week, I became weaker. I could no longer go to work, so I contacted the bank and advised them that I would have to take sick leave until this bug cleared up.

The first day I was off work, I went down to see my GP again, complaining of the same problem. It was a different doctor and she examined my stomach and found it to be ok. However, as I felt unwell, she decided that I would get a sick note and be off work for the remainder of the week. My condition kept getting worse, another week passed and once again I contacted my own GP, who eventually referred me to a specialist in the local hospital. Because there had been no improvement after four weeks, I got an appointment immediately. When I went to the hospital, the specialist questioned me about my illness. They ran some tests and said that they would have to send the analysis to the lab and asked me to come back in a week. This I did and they diagnosed ulcerative colitis, which affects the large intestine. They immediately decided to start me on treatment and asked me to come back in ten days for a one-day procedure. This I agreed to do, but within a week I had a phone call from the specialist's secretary to say that the procedure had been postponed for another week. Eventually, after being ill for about six weeks I went for the day-procedure.

They were concerned by the inflammation they found, so immediately admitted me to the hospital. It wasn't until the following week that my sister noticed my stomach was swollen. She contacted the nurse who advised the doctor. They ran some tests but everything seemed to be ok. The following morning, as it was Monday, the nurse on duty asked another surgeon to see me, as my own surgeon was on a week's leave. He immediately ordered an x-ray and the results were alarming. The nurse on the ward told me I'd have to go to theatre that afternoon.

Shortly after that, the surgeon who was looking after me said that the treatment I was on was not working, and that I would need a colostomy immediately. So he referred me to another surgeon, who came to see me a little later and explained, in a gentler manner, exactly what had happened. His name was Mr Stokes, and he said to me, 'Mr McGrath, this morning you were sent for an x-ray and the radiologist came to the theatre when the x-ray was developed, concerned about the result'. It appeared that the colon was very seriously swollen and in danger of perforating which would have had serious consequences; he said they'd have to operate immediately and would do so that afternoon. He explained to me that the operation would take about two and a half to three hours and that I would be returning to a high dependency ward in the same hospital.

That afternoon, all my family and friends came to see me and they were disturbed to hear the news. At about five o'clock I was wheeled away to the theatre. As I was waiting to go into the operating room, a lot of thoughts went through my mind and one of them was - where is God in all this? I remember that when the nurse told me that I had to go to theatre, I said to her, 'I have to leave this situation in the hands of God'. Shortly after that, I was placed on the operating table. What happened was unknown to me until about a week later.

During the operation, when they opened me up, before they managed to remove the intestine, it burst, causing me to be seriously ill with respiratory problems. It was decided that they would have to send me to a bigger hospital which specialised in this type of treatment – Craigavon Area Hospital, where I could be put on a life support machine. My father and family were advised that it was quite serious at that stage. They had me transferred and the following morning the surgeon on duty, seeing that I was still very sick, decided that he would take me back to the theatre. He opened me up again and flushed me out completely. He rang my father and said that in his opinion he thought I would be ok and make a full recovery. I did so slowly; it was touch and go for a few days.

During that time when I was so sick, many, many people prayed for me and my prayers and pilgrimages to Medjugorje over the number of years came into effect. About a week later I was transferred back to Daisy Hill Hospital in Newry, where I slowly made a full recovery. My sisters, father and other family members told me what had happened. It was a depressing number of weeks as I recovered, but again sickness and suffering in itself is part of human life. Our Lady advises us about being open to accepting the cross of sickness in our lives. Sometimes we find it difficult to understand and to see God and make sense of the whole situation. But I have no doubt that during those days when I was seriously ill, God was in the people who were caring for me – the surgeons, the nurses and doctors who aided me to a full recovery; and that God was also present in the many prayers of the people who prayed for me during that time.

After five weeks in hospital I was discharged to recover at home. It took me about seven months to return to work. However, during my period of recovery and recuperation, I visited Lourdes with the diocese on pilgrimage from my local area. I also managed to visit Medjugorje for the anniversary in 2000. When I returned to Medjugorje after six months, I had a couple of nice experiences. One morning while I was at the English Mass sitting among the congregation, an inner voice told me, 'I am so happy that you are here'. It was as if Our Lady herself had touched my heart because I felt a great sense of joy. This happened to me on a number of occasions during that visit.

Towards the end of the week, we came to know that a number of people would be asked to stay behind because the tour operator had overbooked by about fifteen people. They asked for volunteers to stay behind and, since I didn't have any work to go back to and I was still recovering from the operation, I decided to volunteer. Although the guide thought that maybe I wouldn't be fit for the heat, I was able to stay for a second week.

It was on the morning that the group was leaving to go back home and I was left on my own, that I realised I had to get my confidence back as my sickness had left me feeling vulnerable. I got up and went down to the church for the English Mass and was made to feel very much at home there. After the Mass, a gentleman from Scotland told me that one of the local priests was giving a talk down in the conference hall if I would like to attend, and I agreed to do so. He accompanied me on the walk down. While I was there, it was as if Our Lady said to me, 'Sit down and make yourself at home'. That second week in Medjugorje was a confidence building week. As a consequence of that, I received greater healing and returned to work a lot sooner than I had thought.

In this time of sickness and suffering, which no-one can explain, we have to look to the suffering of Jesus and to those who are worse off than ourselves. Three weeks after I came home from hospital, my sister's husband was involved in a serious accident and has since been left in a wheelchair, paralysed from the neck down. This was a great cross for my sister and her children but thankfully it has given her the grace of patience and empathy, and it has given her a lot of strength as well. It's hard to understand why we suffer these sicknesses and accidents, and there's no point in looking for explanations, but Our Lady does tell us to be open to the suffering of others and of ourselves, and not to see sickness as a curse but rather to see it as a cross and embrace it. In another message, Our Lady invites us to surrender ourselves and our crosses and sorrows, so that she can turn them into joy.

Pray until prayer becomes a joy for you

Medjugorje Message, November 25, 1999
'Dear children! Also today I call you to prayer. In this time of grace, may the Cross be a sign-post of love and unity for you, through which true peace comes. That is why, little children, pray especially at this time that little Jesus, the Creator of peace, may be born in your hearts. Only through prayer will you become my apostles of peace in this world without peace. That is why, pray until prayer becomes a joy for you. Thank you for having responded to my call.'

As children, most of us are taught how to pray by our parents and are brought to Mass on Sundays. My first experience of prayer was when I was brought to Mass in the local St Catherine's Dominican church in Newry. As a small young boy at the time, this building seemed very big and the crowds of people enormous. I had little understanding of what the Mass was about, but was brought there by my parents as part of the family. It wasn't until I went to school in Dublin that my prayer life began to take shape and become more knowledgeable. In the school in Dublin we regularly attended Masses and we were taught morning and night prayers. We were also taught how to pray the Rosary.

I remember when we were at the junior school in Mount Merrion as small children, in the dormitory we asked the house lady if we could we pray the Rosary with her. She was quite reluctant to teach us but agreed in the end. So the suggestion was that we use our fingers to count the decades and she introduced them. When I moved over to the more senior school in Drumcondra, run by the Rosminian Fathers, the Rosary was part of the format of the school. Each evening after supper we assembled in the church for the recitation of the Rosary. Each of the boys – junior, intermediate and senior – had their turn reciting month by month. Also common was the devotion to the Benediction of the Most Blessed Sacrament, particularly on a Thursday, and usually in May and October you had the devotions which included the Rosary and the Benediction. During the time of the old Latin Mass at St Joseph's in Dublin, the vernacular to the new Mass itself was introduced, in 1971 / 72. When the new Mass in its present form was introduced in English we were taught quite a lot about it in school. We used to go to Mass in the mornings on Monday, Wednesday and Friday, and of course at the weekends as well.

When I left the school in Drumcondra, I found myself breaking away from the form of prayer that I had been introduced to. However as I said in an earlier chapter, when I started to work and make my own life, prayer began to become part of my life again. It started at the end of a pilgrimage to Lourdes in 1982, when a priest of the Holy Ghost Fathers was leading the pilgrimage and he encouraged us to take up the recitation of the Rosary on a daily basis. His way of doing so was to say, 'It only takes about fifteen to twenty minutes'. I gave this serious thought and after that pilgrimage began to persevere to pray the Rosary every day. At first this was a bit of a struggle, but the more I kept at it the easier it got, although it took several years before it finally became easy.

As time passed, I felt myself being led to go to Mass every day, which I started to do back in 1983 and thankfully have been able to do so ever since. I also found that the Rosary itself led me back to the sacrament of Confession. This is an example of the way Our Lady has invited the pilgrims and the people of Medjugorje to develop their prayer life.

On the eighth day of the apparition, Father Jozo Zovko, who was the parish priest in Medjugorje at the time, was praying for guidance when he heard an inner voice instructing him to go to the door and to protect the children. Opening the door of the church he found the children 'swarming like bees around him' saying, 'Help us the police are chasing us'. Father Jozo put them into a room which he then locked. He met the police outside; they asked him if he had seen the children. He said yes, that they had gone in 'that direction', and pointed away from the church. As this had happened in response to Father Jozo's prayer for guidance, he decided that a Mass would be introduced in order to pray for more guidance, regarding the authenticity of the apparitions.

At that evening's Mass, Father Jozo said to the people, 'We are in a serious position, we need to pray for guidance'. He invited the parish to fast and they all agreed. So Father Jozo said that they would fast the next day and the day after and the day after that. As Father Jozo described it, the people replied that yes they would fast. So the people of the parish left the church that evening with the intention of fasting, and they all did so. The following evening Father Jozo told the people that if anyone was sick they could take water, but they refused. After the third day, people came for Confession. Father Jozo said, 'Our habits were wet with their tears, the people were repenting of their sins and we had to hear confessions all of that day and that night'. They had to draft more priests from parishes around Medjugorje to hear the confessions. This was one clear example of the answer to Father Jozo's prayer, the guidance that he needed concerning the apparitions at Medjugorje, to ensure that they were from God.

It was after these eight days of the apparitions that the form of the evening programme in Medjugorje began to take shape. The programme would begin with one part of the Rosary, usually the Joyful, Sorrowful or Glorious Mysteries. That would be followed by the Mass at 6pm. In March 1984 Our Lady, through the visionaries, asked that all three parts of the Rosary were said. When the visionaries went to the priests of Medjugorje parish and told them that this instruction had been given to them by Our Lady, the priests wondered amongst themselves how they were going to fit it in. In a later message, Our Lady suggested that they say the Joyful and the Sorrowful mysteries before Mass, so that they could prepare properly to receive Jesus in the Eucharist. After Mass they would pray for healing and say the Glorious Mysteries and thanksgiving. This is the format of the Evening Prayer Programme at Medjugorje today.

In the summertime the Rosary commences at six o'clock, usually starting with the Joyful Mysteries. In between each decade, a verse or chorus of a hymn is followed by the introduction to a decade by the priest in different languages. This is followed by the Sorrowful Mysteries. At about twenty minutes to seven, there's usually a pause to greet the Gospa, Our Lady Queen of Peace, who appears to the visionaries around that time, now in their homes and sometimes in the Adoration Church, but never in the church in public, as the bishop of Mostar has refused permission. However, Our Lady did advise the visionaries that during that time of prayer, the people should be praying in the church and that Our Lady blesses the people in the church even though she doesn't appear to the visionaries there. The Rosary is followed by the Litany of the Blessed Virgin Mary, which is sung in the local Croatian language, followed by a prayer to the Holy Spirit. The Hymn of Medjugorje then intones the beginning of the Mass. The daily Mass in Croatia usually takes about an hour, with profound preaching during the Mass about the messages, and testimonies from witnesses to the conversion of people in Medjugorje at the time. After the Mass there is a set of prayers – the Creed, and seven times the Our Father, Hail Mary and Glory Be to the Father.

One of the visionaries, Vicka Ivankovic, who had had a lot of sickness and suffering herself, had been chosen to pray for sick and suffering people. On the fourth day of the apparition, Vicka's grandmother suggested she take some holy water to the apparition, sprinkle it on Our Lady and say, 'If you're not from Heaven go, but if you are stay'. Vicka did as her grandmother asked, and when she sprinkled the holy water, Our Lady smiled. Vicka began to pray seven times the Our Father, Hail Mary and Glory Be to the Father. Our Lady again smiled and said, 'That is a good prayer, and now I want you to add the Creed, because there are many non-believers nowadays'.

So this set of prayers is prayed at the end of the Mass every evening, and Our Lady invites us to meditate on the five wounds of Our Lord on the cross and to offer the prayer for the intentions of the Pope and thanksgiving. After this the religious articles are blessed, followed by the prayer for the healing of sick people, healing of sickness of mind, body and spirit, again we will discuss this in a later chapter. This is followed by the Glorious Mysteries; thanksgiving for the gift of Jesus in the Eucharist - present within us. This is the format of the prayers that take place every day in Medjugorje. Along with this there is the Adoration of the Most Blessed Sacrament on Wednesday and Saturday evenings in the summertime, usually from ten to eleven.

We Catholics believe that at holy Mass the bread and wine are transubstantiated by the words that the priest uses at the consecration, 'Take this, all of you, and eat it. This is my body'. The same applies to the wine, 'Take this, all of you and drink it. This is the cup of my blood, the blood of the new and everlasting covenant. It will be shed for you and for all, so that sins may be forgiven'.

These are the words that Christ Himself used at the last supper when he introduced the Eucharist to the apostles, and in turn the apostles have introduced it to us, down through the centuries. The Mass is the centre of prayer life in Medjugorje and of the Church. It is the greatest prayer. Our Lady Herself invites us to attend Mass every day if possible but if not, then as often as possible. Our Lady asked the visionaries, 'If you had the choice to come to an apparition or to go to holy Mass, which would you choose?' The visionaries responded, 'We would come to you, Blessed Mother'. Our Lady said, 'No, do not do that, go to holy Mass. You cannot comprehend the greatness of the holy Mass'. So this is the greatest prayer that we as Catholics have, and at the Mass there is the real presence of Jesus in the Eucharist.

Adoration is an extension of the Mass. What happens is that the choir or music group – who are called Cenacolo, and are made up of a number of rehabilitated drug addicts from the local community and founded by Italian nun Sister Elvira - they intone the music. This is part of the fruits of Medjugorje, which we'll come back to at a later stage. The priest comes out on to the altar and goes to the tabernacle. He then removes a large host and places it on the Monstrance. With a congregation in the hundreds or even thousands, sometimes the church is so packed that it's hard to find space at all to sit and most have to stand. The priest offers a little reflection, which is translated into several different languages. Then there's a silent pause and the music is taken up again.

The greatness of the Adoration is overpowering, and quite often you can feel the peace of Christ in the church. Nobody minds standing for an hour. I've done it myself many a time and it's something that we are very grateful for, to be able to be present for the Adoration. This form of Adoration was introduced by the late Father Slavko Barbaric who was the spiritual director of the visionaries and worked in Medjugorje from 1982 until his death in November 2000. His dedication to the whole message of Medjugorje was seen in his example.

So the power of prayer itself is seen as something we can never comprehend or understand, but during the time of prayer in Medjugorje many conversions take place. During the Rosary each evening in Medjugorje, the Sacrament of Confession is also made available in the confessional area outside the church. To the left of the church are a number of small confession boxes and priests hear confession in many different languages. Also, the numbers of people who flock to Medjugorje for Confession means that the priests also have to hear confessions in the outside yard, where signposts direct the penitents to the appropriate box for their own language.

Confession is a part of the message of Medjugorje; Our Lady invites us to confess at least once a month. Many of us have great difficulty with this sacrament, but it is a form of prayer and penance. The difficulty is that we find it hard to come to terms with our guilt and we are frightened of our sinfulness and weaknesses. It was through the Rosary and going to Mass that I found myself being able to practise frequent confession, sometimes as often as once a week, but usually about once a fortnight. I find the sacrament of confession a very reviving form of spirituality. It takes away all the little rickety bits that you carry about in your heart and mind, and you feel as if you have given the soul a great bath of refreshment, of the blood and water of the sacrament, the mercy that flows from the wound of the side of Christ.

Many have difficulty with this sacrament, but Our Lady says that there is not one human being on this earth who does not need monthly confession. In Medjugorje, queues can be seen of those wanting to go to confession. Many people who come to Medjugorje have been away from the sacrament for years – some as much as forty or fifty years. I remember a gentleman in one of our groups once, who hadn't been to confession for nearly sixty years, but was able to find the grace to confess at Medjugorje. There have been many great conversions and I have no doubt that this is through the prayer programme that takes place each day, and of course the great presence of Our Lady and her divine Son.

When I first started to pray the rosary first back in 1982, I found it very difficult. In fact I always found prayer a great chore or even sometimes boring! It wasn't until I first went to Medjugorje back in 1986 that I realised that praying the rosary had a very deep meaning for me, as if I was praying to somebody who was very close to me. Since then I have been able to pray with great ease, but it still takes perseverance. Medjugorje is known as the school of prayer, but at this school there are no weekend breaks or bank holidays – it's a daily school. Our Lady invites us to pray with openness, to pray and express ourselves and then prayer becomes a joy for us. Not only is Our Lady inviting us to say prayers, but also to allow the prayer in our lives and the spirit of God to grow within us. This can be found in how we express ourselves and how we treat one another.

Over the years, I've found that my prayer life has enabled me to be gentler and more considerate towards other people. It has healed my attitude; I used to be short tempered at times. I've also found that it has helped me to grow in love and respect for those in my family, and those I work with, as well as strangers I meet on the street.

Sometimes we don't feel so great going to work in the morning Recently, I was travelling to work on the train on my own and I remember feeling a bit tired and groggy, not feeling the best. However, when I got to my work and I began to start, I realised that I was expressing myself in a joyful way while speaking to others. Then I knew that the spirit of prayer was coming alive within me. On another occasion, many years ago when I was working in Newry, it was a busy morning and things were getting on top of me a bit. However I was able to express myself to those around me with a great sense of joy. The manager of the branch recognised this and was surprised to see me so joyful and happy in what I was doing, even though I was under extreme pressure. I have no doubt that I was helped by the presence of Our Lady there. It was prayer becoming a joy, not just for me but for those around me.

Prayer itself is a grace. Many of us find it difficult because we don't have the grace to pray, but if we don't start we will never be able to pray. In another message Our Lady said, 'You want to hear the messages but you don't want to get started'. If we don't start to pray and if we don't persevere in prayer then prayer becomes meaningless, and that's why so many people today only want to pray when they need something, or in a time of an emergency; this is what Our Lady does not want. Our Lady says in another message that our prayer should become a daily encounter with God.

Medjugorje Message, November 25, 1988

'Dear children! I call you to prayer, to have an encounter with God in prayer. God gives Himself to you, but He wants you to respond freely to His invitation. That is why, little children, you should find yourselves a special time during the day, when you can pray in peace and humility, and have this meeting with God the creator. I am with you and I intercede for you in front of God. Be vigilant, so that every encounter in prayer will be the joy of your contact with God. Thank you for having responded to my call.'

So it is a joyful encounter with God, not just begging from God; prayer is like a relationship with God. We all like to have relationships and friendships with other people but Our Lady invites us to take her hand and allow her to lead us to her divine son. That is where she's going to lead us, nowhere else; away from sin and into the arms of her divine son. My suggestion for those who are not praying - as well as those who are contemplating a life of daily prayer - is to begin by praying the Rosary. The Rosary is made up of four parts; recently the late Pope John Paul II introduced new mysteries called the Luminous Mysteries or the Mysteries of Light.

The Joyful Mysteries

1. The Annunciation, where the Angel Gabriel announces God's message to Mary that she is to become the mother of His son. Mary expresses her acceptance in the following words, 'I am the handmaid of the Lord'.

2. The Visitation, where Mary goes to visit her cousin Saint Elizabeth, having been told by the angel that she was in her sixth month of pregnancy, Mary stays for three months to help Elizabeth. That joyful encounter, the meeting of Mary and Saint Elizabeth, was something that John the Baptist himself experienced when he recognised his saviour in his mother's womb. Jesus was only three days old when John the Baptist leapt for joy.

3. The Birth of Our Lord, where Mary brings forth her first son and wraps Him in swaddling clothes at the great feast of Christmas.

4. The Presentation, where Jesus is presented by Joseph and Mary at forty days old as part of the Jewish custom and religion. Jesus is brought to the temple and presented to God, to whom an offering is made on his behalf. The old priest Simeon said to Mary, 'This child is destined to bring about the rise and fall of

many in Israel, destined to be a sign, to be rejected and to be a sword that will pierce your own soul, so that the secret thoughts of many hearts will be made to bear'. Simeon was prophesying the passion and death of Our Lord.

5. The Finding of Jesus in the Temple. This is the last of the Joyful Mysteries, where Jesus goes missing on a journey back home from the Jewish Passover in Jerusalem and his parents search for him for three days, after which they find him and are joyfully reunited with him. His mother anxiously asked why he had done this and he replied, 'Did you not know that I must be about My Father's affairs?' However, they did not understand what he meant by this. Jesus went back to Nazareth and lived obediently under their authority, 'And Jesus grew in wisdom and stature, and in favour of God and men.' (Luke 2:52)

The Mysteries of Light

1. The Baptism of Jesus in the river Jordon, where John the Baptist has the privilege of baptising Jesus in the waters that were made holy by the one he was baptising.

2. The First Miracle of Jesus at the wedding of Cana, where, at the request of his mother, Jesus turns eight jugs of water into wine.

3. The Proclamation of the Kingdom of God, where Jesus goes into various towns, proclaims that the Kingdom of God is near at hand, and invites us to convert. This word 'convert' you could say is the main theme of the apparitions at Medjugorje. It is used quite a lot by Our Lady.

4. The Transfiguration, where Jesus takes Peter, John and James up the high mountain and at the summit He is transformed into the likeness of the sun. He speaks with Moses and Elijah, and Peter says, 'It's wonderful for us to be here; let's build three tents, one for You, one for Elijah and one for Moses'. A cloud covers them and the voice of the Father is heard to say, 'This is my beloved Son, in whom I am well pleased'.

5. Jesus introduces the Eucharist to the Apostles, which we have already covered in this chapter.

The Sorrowful Mysteries, where the passion and death of Our Lord take place.

1. The Garden of Gethsemane. After the last supper Jesus takes his disciples here. Then he leads Peter, James and John deeper into the garden than the others, where he says, 'Stay here and keep watch over me; pray not to be put to the test because the spirit is willing but the flesh is weak'. Jesus goes about a stone's throw away to a spot where he begins to pray, 'Father if it were possible may this cup of suffering pass from me; nevertheless let it be not as I but as you would have it'. Jesus then realises that he is about to endure the greatest passion and death for our sins. He willingly accepts the suffering from the Father. Jesus is arrested and betrayed by Judas. He is locked up and questioned by the authorities, and Pilot has him scourged.

2. Jesus is scourged. We quite often offer this mystery in atonement for the sins of mankind. Mary and the women look on as Jesus is scourged at the pillar. This is portrayed very well in the film of The Passion of the Christ.

3. Jesus is mocked and crowned with thorns. The thorns are pressed into the skull so that they

penetrate and cause great laceration, pain and bleeding. The soldiers spit on him and mock him. Quite often we do that in our own lives – we spit upon Jesus when we spit upon each other and abuse and ridicule each other.

4. Jesus is led up to Calvary, carrying that heavy wooden cross on his shoulder, where he falls three times.

5. The Crucifixion and the death of Jesus on the cross.

However three days later we come to the Glorious Mysteries where Jesus overpowers death.

1. The Resurrection, where the women go to prepare and anoint the body for final burial. When they arrive, they find that the body has gone, and an Angel tells them, 'He is not here, He has risen'. The women go and tell the disciples, who refuse to believe them, and eventually Jesus appears to them all.

2. The Ascension, where Jesus takes the disciples to the mountain once again, then parts with them and ascends into Heaven - blessing them and instructing them, 'Go and make disciples of all nations, baptise them in

the name of the Father and of the Son and of the Holy Spirit, I am with you always'. The disciples fearfully go to the upper room and prepare to wait for the coming of the Holy Spirit, the third Glorious Mystery.

3. The Holy Spirit comes down upon the church - the feast of Pentecost. We should continuously pray to the Holy Spirit, as Our Lady says in the messages each day, 'Pray to the Holy Spirit, the Holy Spirit will inspire and guide us in the proper way of life'. The disciples gather in the upper room with Mary and other women who lead them in prayer. The Holy Spirit came upon them in tongues of fire and without fear they went out and started to preach in Jerusalem and proclaim that Jesus Christ, the one who they crucified, had risen.

The fourth and fifth mysteries concern Mary herself.

4. The Assumption of Our Lady into Heaven, where Mary - who was born free from sin and who carried the Saviour – was taken up into Heaven with her soul. No decay was allowed to touch her body, which was assumed. She is now united with her son.

5. The Coronation, where Mary is crowned Queen of Heaven and Earth. Today she comes as Queen of Peace, Our Lady says, 'I am the Queen of Peace; I have come to convert and reconcile'.

These are the mysteries of the Rosary. I have spoken a lot in this chapter about the Rosary because it has been the prayer that has helped me to form a spiritual life throughout these twenty or so years, and to appreciate the sacraments of the Eucharist and Confession. The Rosary also, as Our Lady says, helps us to prepare for Mass properly and to have a deeper appreciation of our faith. The Rosary will guard us in our faith and will help protect and reaffirm our faith, which is very important. Many people today simply don't know what to believe in, so they don't believe in anything. The Rosary is a first step that I would recommend to anyone who is considering taking up praying. It's not easy to pray but it does get easier.

As a person who is visually impaired, I find the Rosary my form of scripture and my bible as well. The Rosary helps me to picture the events that are revealed in it. It has helped me to have a deeper understanding and love for the Mass itself, and has strengthened my faith in the real presence of Jesus. It also protects me from sin; helping me to remove the bad habits of sin in my life. Quite often it's easy to fall back into our own routine of bad habits and sometimes they're sinful habits that are hard to get out of. It's clear to me that prayer is the only way to overcome any sinful weaknesses that we have in life, and I've found the Rosary very beneficial in this respect. When I do commit serious sin, which thankfully is not too often, Our Lady gently guides me to Confession; this is what Our Lady does. She never condemns anybody and neither does her Son, but they simply invite us to confess our sins and be open to the forgiveness and compassion of Jesus. This is what always happens in Medjugorje, when the sacrament of the Eucharist and the sacrament of Confession are made available to the pilgrims who go there.

At this point it might be advisable to reflect upon some of the messages which Our Lady has communicated to us through the visionaries, concerning the greatness of the holy Mass.

Medjugorje Message, April 3, 1986

'Dear children! I wish to call you to live the holy Mass. There are many of you who have sensed the beauty of the Mass, but there are also those who come unwillingly. I have chosen you, dear children, but Jesus gives you His grace in the Mass. Therefore, consciously live the holy Mass and let your coming to it be a joyful one. Come to it with love and make the

Mass your own. Thank you for having responded to my call.'

Medjugorje Message, April 25, 1988
'Dear children! God wants to make you holy. Therefore, through me He is inviting you to completely surrender yourselves. Let the holy Mass be your life. Understand that the church is God's palace, the place in which I gather you to show you the way to God. Come and pray. Neither look to others nor slander them, but rather, let your life be a testimony to the way of holiness. Churches deserve respect and are set apart as holy because God, who became man, dwells in them day and night. Therefore, little children, believe and pray that the Father increases your faith, and then ask for whatever you need. I am with you and I am rejoicing because of your conversion and protecting you with my motherly mantle. Thank you for having responded to my call.'

Medjugorje Message, January 25, 1998
'Dear children! Today again I call all of you to prayer. Only with prayer, dear children, will your heart change, become better, and be more sensitive to the Word of God. Little children, do not permit Satan to pull you apart and to do with you what he wants. I call you to be responsible and determined and to consecrate each day to God in prayer. May holy

Mass, little children, not be a habit for you, but a way of life. By living holy Mass each day, you will feel the need for holiness and you will grow in holiness. I am close to you and intercede before God for each of you, so that He may give you strength to change your heart. Thank you for having responded to my call.'

I wish to say a few things concerning the Mass, as it has been part of my life for twenty six years. I first started going to daily Mass in 1983. I used to find it a bit boring, particularly the Old Testament, but now I know that every part of the Mass is extremely important; the Old Testament, the New Testament and the actions of the priest. The Mass is made up of four parts: the Penitential Rite; the Liturgy of the Word; the Liturgy of the Eucharist and the Concluding Rite. We can say our Rosary or Way of the Cross or whatever prayers we choose to say, but we cannot have the Mass without the priest, who has been chosen by God and anointed on his day of ordination. He is not like a doctor or a lawyer or any other profession; he is chosen to represent us the people, and to offer the sacrifice of the Mass on our behalf. A priest is also chosen to become like Christ himself, so that during Mass he can offer himself totally with Christ in union with his suffering and death on the cross.

We shall at this point go through the Mass itself as it is in the New Rite. The first part of the Mass, when the priest enters the altar, is his climb to Calvary; on our behalf he represents Christ who is offering himself as a victim for our sins. The Priest begins the Mass with the words, 'The grace of our Lord Jesus Christ and the love of God and the fellowship of the Holy Spirit be with you' and we respond, 'And with your spirit.' We come then to the Penitential Rite, when the priest invites us to acknowledge our sinfulness and our failures, and we do this as we say the Confiteor, the 'I Confess'. In that prayer, we confess that we have sinned in thought, word and deed, and ask the Blessed Mary, all the angels and saints and the congregation to pray for us. That is where the community at Mass pray for one another.

It's important to point out that Our Lady also said that the journey from our house to the church, by car or on foot, should be a prayer. Every time we go to church, it's a step out in faith. As we move on in the Liturgy of the Mass, the readings are usually taken from the Old Testament, or sometimes, such as during the season of Easter, they're taken from the Acts of the Apostles, which are about the early days of the Church. Then the priest or deacon reads the Gospel, which is the word of Christ – the New Testament. This is where we have to listen very attentively. We can also find links between the Old and New

Testaments when we carefully study the scripture. Usually on a Sunday the priest gives a reflection or a homily on the Gospel or the readings of that day. This is also an important part of the Mass, because we, the faithful, need the Holy Spirit, and the Holy Spirit works through the priest to guide and direct us.

Then we come to the Profession of Faith, where we the faithful and the priests confess our faith in the Trinity: the Father, Son and Holy Spirit. This is done not only in words, but must also be seen in actions in our daily life. We come then to the Prayers of the Faithful, where the priest offers prayers on behalf of all the faithful who are present, as well as those in the church as a whole throughout the world. The Offertory of the Mass is where the priest offers the bread and wine on our behalf. In this part of the Mass we are all united, as the priest sprinkles water, which represents the congregation, into the wine. This is followed by the Preface, and prepares us for the Eucharistic Prayer, which is said prior to the Sanctus - the Holy Holy.

Now we move onto the Eucharistic prayer, so let us reflect on that for a moment. There are five Eucharistic prayers, the first four of which are most commonly used at Mass. The fifth one, which is used less often, is known as the Penitential Rite Eucharistic Prayer. I would like to reflect now on Eucharistic

Prayer number three. The Priest opens that prayer by saying, 'Father you are holy indeed and all creation rightly gives you praise. All life, all holiness comes from you through your son Jesus Christ our Lord by the working of the Holy Spirit. From age to age you gather the people to yourself so that from east to west, a perfect offering may be made to the glory of your name, and so Father we bring you these gifts'. At this point the priest extends his hands over the gifts and says, 'We ask you to make them holy by the power of your Spirit, that they may become for us the Body and the Blood of your son our Lord Jesus Christ'. The priest then begins the Consecration saying, 'The night before he died, he broke bread, gave it to his disciples and said,

'TAKE THIS ALL OF YOU AND EAT IT, THIS IS MY BODY WHICH WILL BE GIVEN UP FOR YOU'

The priest elevates the host which is now the Body of Christ. Here I would suggest you say a quiet prayer, 'Jesus I believe that you are truly present and I offer my unworthy self up to you', and bow gently as the priest elevates the host for the congregation to adore. After that, the priest places the host back on the paten and genuflects. He lifts the cup and says, 'When supper was ended, Jesus took the cup, again he gave

You thanks and praise, gave the cup to his disciples and said,

'TAKE THIS ALL OF YOU AND DRINK FROM IT, THIS IS THE CUP OF MY BLOOD, THE BLOOD OF THE NEW AND EVERLASTING COVENANT, IT WILL BE SHED FOR YOU AND FOR ALL, SO THAT SINS MAY BE FORGIVEN. DO THIS IN MEMORY OF ME'

At this point the priest elevates the chalice containing the precious blood. It is always advisable here to bow again, in adoration of the presence of Jesus. He places the chalice back on the altar and genuflects again. The priest says to the congregation, 'Let us proclaim the mystery of faith', and we usually respond with the Acclamation of Faith, which for Eucharistic prayer number three would be, 'When we eat this bread and drink from this cup, we proclaim your death Lord Jesus until you come in glory'. The priest carries on with the Eucharistic Prayer, saying, 'Father, calling to mind the death your Son endured for our salvation, his glorious resurrection and ascension into heaven, and ready to greet him when he comes again, we offer you in thanksgiving this holy and living sacrifice'. At this point, bear in mind that you're offering the body and blood of Jesus back to his Father.

Then, 'May this sacrifice which has made our peace with you, advance the peace and salvation of all the world. Strengthen in faith and love your pilgrim Church on earth; your servant Pope and Bishops, clergy and faithful'. This is followed by the Intercessory Prayer for the dead, 'Remember Lord our brothers and sisters who have gone to their rest in the hope of rising again. Bring them and all the faithful departed into the light of your presence'. Finally, the priest prays for the entire world, 'Have mercy on us all; make us worthy to share eternal life with Mary the virgin mother of God, the apostles, the martyrs and all the saints who have done your will throughout the ages. May we praise you in union with them and give you glory through your son Jesus Christ'.

The priest raises the paten, containing the Body of Christ, and the chalice, and says the Doxology Prayer, which should be said only by the priest and not the faithful, 'Through him with him and in him, in the unity of the Holy Spirit, all glory and honour is yours almighty Father, forever and ever', and we the faithful respond, 'Amen', which means, I agree with everything that has taken place at that point in the Mass. The priest invites the faithful to stand and pray the Our Father – the prayer that Jesus himself taught us. As we pray the Our Father, we should focus on the meaning of what we are saying. Then the priest prays the Prayer of Deliverance, 'Deliver us Lord from every evil, and grant us peace in our day. In your mercy keep us free from sin, and protect us from all anxiety, as we wait in joyful hope for the coming of our saviour Jesus Christ', and the faithful respond, 'For the kingdom, the power and the glory are yours, now and forever'.

The priest extends his hands over the faithful and prays the following prayer, which again should only be said by the priest, as has been laid down in the Rite of the Mass, 'Lord Jesus Christ, you said to your apostles, "I leave you peace, my peace I give you". Look not on our sins but on the faith of your Church, and grant us the peace and unity of your kingdom, where you live forever and ever', and we again respond, 'Amen'. The priest then says to the congregation, 'The peace of Christ the Lord be with you all', and we would say, 'And with your spirit'. The priest now invites the congregation to offer a sign of peace – usually by shaking hands. The priest takes the Host, he breaks it over the chalice and says the following prayer, 'May this mingling of the Body and Blood of our Lord Jesus Christ bring eternal life to us who receive it'. Then he invites the congregation to pray the Lamb of God, which is acknowledging the presence of Jesus as the Lamb of God and asking for mercy upon us and the world. We kneel, and the priest elevates the host again, and says to the congregation, 'This is the Lamb of God, who takes away the sins of the world. Happy are those who are called to his supper', and we respond, 'Lord, I am not worthy to receive you, but only say the word and my soul shall be healed'. At that point, the priest himself receives the precious Body and Blood of Jesus through the Eucharist, and I usually say the following prayers, which would quite often be said by priests.

The first one I normally say at this point is, 'Lord Jesus Christ, son of the living God, by the will of the Father and work of the Holy Spirit, your death brought life to the world, and by your holy Body and Blood, free me from all my sins and from every evil. Keep me faithful to your teaching and never let me be parted from you'.

The second one is, 'Lord Jesus Christ, with faith in your love and mercy, I eat your Body and drink your Blood. Let it not bring me condemnation but health in mind and in body'.

At this point in the Mass, the distribution of Holy Communion takes place. There are a few conditions laid down for receiving Holy Communion and I think it's worth pointing them out here. The first one is that we come up to Holy Communion with reverence, and dressed in a tidy manner, so that we can receive the Lord with dignity and respect. We are free to receive

Holy Communion either on the tongue or in the hands, whichever one feels comfortable with. We are also free to kneel if we wish or to stand. The second condition is that we must have fasted from all food, with the exception of water for medicinal purposes, for one hour before the receiving Holy Communion. That is not before the beginning of Mass, but before the receiving Holy Communion. The third condition is that we must be in a state of grace. This means that we must not have committed mortal sin. If we commit mortal sin, we must attend the sacrament of Confession before receiving Holy Communion. At this point let us consider what the terms of committing mortal sin are. There are three: full consent, full commitment and full knowledge. If these three criteria are met, you have committed mortal sin.

What sins substantiate mortal sins? First of all, if we break any of the Ten Commandments under the three conditions, for instance if we refuse to attend Mass on a Sunday or Holy days of Obligation, as Church law clearly states the commandment of God to keep holy the Sabbath day. The Church recommends that we attend Mass every Sunday. Failure to do so with full knowledge, full consent and full commitment amounts to mortal sin. Again I'd say to people, if one falls into mortal sin it is important to seek Confession as soon as possible, because one doesn't know the time of one's death. But I've no doubt that people can get to confession as quickly as possible, because you cannot go to Holy Communion in a state of mortal sin.

These are the conditions laid down for us to receive Holy Communion. After receiving Holy Communion, there may be a short pause. The priest then says the Concluding Prayer and performs the blessing of the congregation, before descending from the altar, genuflecting and finally leaving the altar. At this point the Mass is ended. We can of course say our own personal prayers, but there are none greater than the sacrifice of the holy Mass. I've often heard people say, 'Ah well, I say my own prayers at home, so I don't need to go to Mass'. You know, it's an act of faith to be able to leave your home in order to attend Mass. Of all the prayers that people could say, the greatest prayer is the Mass and Our Lady points that out very clearly in this message:

Medjugorje Message, 1983
'The Mass is the greatest prayer of God. You will never be able to understand its greatness. That is why you must be perfectly humble at Mass, and you should prepare yourselves for it.'

In the Mass we are not only praying for ourselves, but also for the wider community, the sick, and for world communities as well. During Mass, we are stating that we are part of that community of faith, by our witness and example. We are also praying for the faithful departed, which could be our parents, our grandparents, our friends, brothers or sisters. They could also be the souls detained in purgatory. So whatever prayers we say, if we don't attend the holy Mass, or make an effort to attend, then simply saying our own private prayers at home will not be very beneficial. I think that, when we pray and attend Mass, it's important to remember that we are also praying for others, not only for our own community, but for the entire Church throughout the world. Also, when we pray the rosary, in the second part of the Hail Mary we're also praying for the entire world, as we say, 'Holy Mary, Mother of God pray for us sinners', that's the entire human race, not just the Catholic world or the Christian world, but the unbelieving world as well.

That is the power of prayer, and it's important for us to be able to live what we learn at Mass. The Eucharist itself gives us the strength to be joyful witnesses to the presence of God in our places of work, our families, our homes, and in the wider community. We might often think to ourselves that our prayers aren't answered or we don't receive guidance. I wish to share with you a few short stories of my own, where I have found guidance in prayer. Sometimes, when we go to the Sacrament of

Confession, we aren't aware of what the priest is saying, or we don't always pay much attention to it. I think it's important that we do pay attention to whatever the priest has to say to us in confession. This was made clear to me in the following situation.

One day, I went to confession in my own parish in Newry, and the priest, after hearing my confession, told me that he wanted me to pray for guidance for this period in my life. So I prayed for guidance and then thought nothing more of it. However, a few days later at work, my boss told me that I would have to accept a transfer to the Belfast branch or face redundancy. I only had a day or so to make the decision, so I said that I would need to pray and think about it. That night when I came home, I decided to say the third part of the rosary and ask for guidance about the decision I had to make. Later that night, I received the guidance, which was to try the job in Belfast. Thankfully, it worked out, and I'm still in that situation of employment, as a consequence.

On another occasion I was heading to Medjugorje for Christmas. At five thirty in the morning I was in the departure check-in area at Dublin airport, not knowing which desk to go to and trying to find somebody who could answer a question. The place was so crowded that it was almost impossible to move. I quietly asked for the assistance of Our Lady by saying a short Hail Mary. I found myself moving in one direction, not knowing exactly where I was going, but ended up at the correct check-in desk. When I got to security, it was very busy as well. Again I called on Our Lady, and the supervisor of the queue, seeing that I had a visual impairment, came and took me up to the front of the queue. So I got through security quite quickly, in time for my flight. Eventually I found myself on board the correct flight, and I have no doubt that was also through the assistance of Our Lady.

One bank holiday weekend, when I needed to post some items to Dublin urgently, I didn't think I had the correct stamps and I was worried that they wouldn't get there in time. While I was praying the rosary in my room, it came to me that the stamps that I needed were in my winter coat, and that there were envelopes big enough to send the items down to Dublin. I was further instructed that I could get a cheque in a local exchange bureau, to change my Sterling into Euros. The inspiration I had during the rosary turned out to be correct, and when I followed its guidance, everything worked out.

It's important, as we close this chapter, to note that prayer is an essential element of our spiritual growth, helping us to detach ourselves from the things of this world, and to grow more and more towards the things of heaven. As the words of the hymn go, 'Turn your eyes towards Jesus, look full in his wonderful face, and then the things of earth will grow strangely dim, in the glory and the light of God's grace'.

Afterword

I first met Patrick on the platform at Belfast Central train station, where we struck up a conversation while figuring out which of the approaching trains would take us home to Newry that evening. During that journey home I found out about Patrick's passion for Medjugorje – a place that I had never heard of, or at least had not registered in my conscious mind. Patrick was astonished that a Catholic from his home town approaching forty years of age would not have any idea that this place even existed! During the journeys to and from work over the next couple of years, I was to hear a lot of the amazing stories Patrick had to tell about managing his life with very little eyesight and about how he became a regular visitor to Medjugorje. After a while, I asked Patrick if he'd ever thought about writing a book, he said that he had but that his disability would make that difficult. I loaned Patrick my voice recorder so that he could get the process underway.

Patrick handed over two audio tapes to me containing the first eight chapters of this book, and during these last few years I've found it difficult to make progress. At one point I had to admit to Patrick that I was not able to put my hand on tape number one, which was only half completed. This was news I did not want to impart, but after lots of searching, I had to admit that it may be gone for good, hoping Patrick might be able to reproduce it but knowing what a hard task that would be. I continued on with tape number two, hoping that one day number one would turn up. During Patrick's illness he told me of a third tape he had completed that was in his house somewhere. As time passed I hoped that it hadn't suffered the same fate as number one. I began to think that maybe the book wasn't meant to be after all.

On the night that Patrick died, I was speaking with his family and friends. I mentioned the third tape, and after a quick look upstairs, Patrick's brother found a few. On listening, one of them sounded like Patrick's voice, although a lot more frail at that stage. I said goodnight to Patrick, letting him know that we had found number three. The next day, waking up in the knowledge that Patrick had passed on to a better place, I was determined to put tape number three somewhere that I would not forget about. Taking it upstairs, I immediately noticed another tape sitting on the dressing table. On playing it I found it to be tape number one! Amazed at this, any doubts I had in my mind about the importance of continuing with the book, completely dissolved. The task of converting these tapes to text became all the more precious when Patrick passed away on 13th December 2011; the day of his fifty-first birthday. Patrick wanted to record one last (fourth) tape to finish this book, which he told me he would use as a kind of goodbye. As time did not allow that to happen I am honoured to bring these chapters to a close.

Thinking back, when Patrick told me that he didn't have long to live, he was careful and considerate, to counter the effect the news would have. Patrick's outlook was inspiring and comforting; he said that when you spend a large part of your life praying that you'll reach eternal life, and then someone tells you it's going to happen soon, there's a certain amount of joy in that. I think it's appropriate to draw this book to a close with the words from Mother Theresa, the reflection reading that Patrick chose for his funeral and that I was privileged to read for him.

Helen Loughran

Anyone is capable of going to heaven

Heaven is our home.
People ask me about death and whether I look forward to it, and I answer, 'Of course', because I am going home.

Dying is not the end, it is just the beginning.
Death is a continuation of life.
This is the meaning of eternal life;
It is where our soul goes to God, to speak to God,
To continue loving him with greater love
Because in Heaven we shall be able to love him
With our whole heart and our soul
Because we surrender our body in death – our heart and our soul live forever.

When we die we are going to be with God,
And with all those we have known who have gone before us; our family and our friends will be there waiting for us.

Heaven must be a beautiful place.
Every religion has an eternity, another life.
People who fear death are the ones who believe this is the end.
I have not known anyone die in fear
If they have witnessed the love of God.

They have to make their peace with God, as do we all.

People die suddenly all the time
So it could happen to us too at any moment.
Yesterday is gone and tomorrow has not yet come,
So we must live each day as if it were our last,
So that when God calls us we are ready
And prepared to die with a clean heart.

Mother Theresa

www.ingramcontent.com/pod-product-compliance
Lightning Source LLC
Chambersburg PA
CBHW061440040426
42450CB00007B/1146